The
Runway

Reflections On The
Ten Commandments

Robert G. Tuttle

CSS Publishing Company, Inc., Lima, Ohio

Library of Congress Cataloging-in-Publication Data

Tuttle, Robert G., 1907-
  The runway : reflections on the Ten Commandments / Robert G. Tuttle.
      p.   cm.
  ISBN 0-7880-0388-7
  1. Ten commandments.   I. Title.
BV4655.T88   1997
241.5'2—dc20   96-38668
                                                                             CIP

ISBN: 0-7880-0388-7   PRINTED IN U.S.A.

Dedicated to

Those who are seeking
a guide to abundant life

Table Of Contents

Introduction

Why *The Runway*? Let's say that I am flying at night alone. It is stormy and I am lost. My fuel is running low. I know that soon I will have to come down through that darkness. But there is no place to land. I am about to give up, when suddenly there is a break in the clouds and there below me is a narrow string of lights. A runway! I can land and live. Thank God.

Would I be angry because the path between the lights is narrow? No! It guides me to life! If I am crazy, I can fly beyond it and die, or fly short of it and die. If I am foolish I can fly to the right of it and crash, or to the left of it and perish. No! I am grateful and I land right on that narrow runway and I live.

That's the straight and narrow way that God has prepared in life for me to follow and live in right relationships. God has prepared a way in life where I can put my life down and live abundantly: the Ten Commandments and the Sermon on the Mount. It may be narrow but it leads straight to life's fulfillment. It does not confine me; it releases me. It directs me. A life of moral obedience made beautiful by the love of Christ. I don't want to miss it. O God, lead me to it and let me live.

At this moment in history our nation and the world are running wild. We are off course. We have forgotten the Ten Commandments and the ways of Christ. Our culture is rapidly becoming secular and anti-religion. If we do not discover our roots, we will soon perish. If we do not find the runway for life that God has established for our safety, we will soon crash. We need to look carefully once more at the Ten Commandments. It is both ancient and modern. God did establish boundaries for humanity — human relationships.

He provided a runway where we can land our lives safely. If we disregard this runway we will crash and perish.

The Ten Commandments are not negative. They suggest a positive way of life. They are sane rules for human relationships. By the grace of God we hope that we will be able to rediscover this very clear way of life that God has provided.

Chapter 1

The Ten Commandments And The "New Morality"

It has been said that "history belongs to the praying people, who believe the future into being." Moses was one who believed the future into being.

After a trip into Eastern Europe, Billy Graham said, "Leaders here are saying they have to have a moral base to their society. They need a moral ideology. They think the best teaching of humanity is the Ten Commandments and the Sermon on the Mount." These two great statements of truth are "God's no and God's yes." We must look seriously at them in our own nation again. If we do not, we will die like a tree whose roots have been cut off. If we do not come to this fresh moral commitment it will be as Norman Mailer describes: "Our inner lives, our inner landscape is just like that sky out there — it's full of smog. We really don't know what we believe anymore, we're nervous about everything."

Our political, industrial, educational, banking, and personal breakdown is the natural fruit of the failure of our homes and schools to teach effectively strong moral structure for life's relationships. Too many of our leaders never have been taught to be honest. We are crashing, off the runway.

Recently a competent university psychiatrist observed: "These persons who come to me need an inner structure for their lives. They need an inner discipline that they themselves have accepted as having the authority of reality. Anyone knows that the Ten Commandments are the best set of rules ever given for an individual to structure his life upon. The problem is that too many people have learned the Ten Commandments and that too few have accepted them as the inner structure of their being."

Now we have to go back to our roots. The children of Israel are standing at the foot of Mount Sinai; Moses has just returned from the presence of God on top of Sinai, bringing with him ten great principles of human relationships. Moses was sensitive to the mind of God and also sensitive to the spiritual needs of human beings. The Ten Commandments outlined a disciplined life for the newly-freed Hebrew slaves. God had something great in mind for this little group of Hebrews. Moses was building for his people an inner discipline that would carry them beyond mere civilization toward a society of justice and love that would be known as the Kingdom of God. Moses saw these commandments as the Word of God. The Christian Church still strives toward this yet unfulfilled dream. Moses made no apology for saying, "Thus saith the Lord!"

A cartoon pictures ancient monks copying the Scriptures: One leans over to a neighbor and says, "Somebody is going to get a break, I just skipped two of the commandments." Most of us have a false concept that it is an expression of freedom to be unaware of moral demands. It is the kind of freedom that turns off all the stop lights and leaves the wreckage piled up at the intersections of life. Moses stated great principles of life clearly and simply. We obey these directions in order that we may find the rich fullness of life in authentic God-to-man and man-to-man relationships.

The Hebrews accepted this: They made it a family affair and instructed their children, line upon line, precept upon precept, coming and going, night and day, from generation to generation; they became a people of character.

Can we be so stupid that we assume that permissiveness is progress? Permissiveness is a throwback to the instincts of the jungle. Don't let us confuse immorality and unfaith with progress; progress has been achieved through enlightened moral concepts, and through faith that God was pulling man up on tiptoe for more adequate living.

We are frightened by negatives; but when a person or a civilization approaches blindly the edge of the precipice, the only loving word is "No!" The intelligent "No!" is the foundation on which the great "yeses" stand. A current of divine life can penetrate a

10

people; this happened to the children of Israel. They broke out into new dimensions of life which were made possible by new disciplines, which gave them specified directions toward greatness. At this moment in history we need to face it: The times are right for a moral and spiritual change of direction.

The Ten Commandments are not blind negatives, cramping the style of full life; they are great affirmatives pointing to the highest expression of life. William Barkley summarizes the Ten Commandments as affirmatives: "Reverence for God and for the name of God; reverence for God's Day; respect for parents; respect for life; respect for property; respect for truth, and for another person's good name; respect for one's self, so wrong desire will never master us."

What is the "New Morality" today? Much of it is *no* morality, no restraints, no norm, no principles: do as you please. This is the old Antinomian Heresy: It has been made modern by contemporary secular existentialism with Jean-Paul Sartre as its prophet. With a little study, we see that this is not the way *up*! It is the way *out*!

However, some expressions of the "New Morality" are responsible. They seek earnestly to give the interpretation of Christian love to the application of dependable life principles. Joseph Fletcher, in his *Situation Ethics,* doesn't advocate permissiveness, but a strenuous observance of the demands of Christian love in our time.

Jesus himself was an advocate of this kind of New Morality. "I came not to destroy the law but to fulfill it," he reminded those who were looking for an easy way out, and added: "Heaven and earth shall pass away but the eternal principles of life's relationships shall not pass away." Jesus did, however, interpret Law according to the highest demands of love. He held to the important principles and despised trivia. Even though he reverenced the Sabbath, he broke it when persons were hungry and when persons needed healing. On the other hand, he refused to open easy loopholes in the great moral principles of the Ten Commandments. He said: "It has been said, thou shalt not kill, but I say unto you, thou

11

shalt not hate thy brother"; he added, "It hath been said, thou shalt not commit adultery, but I say unto you, thou shalt not look with lust upon a woman."

If we want to be honest in dealing with moral and ethical questions, we can accept the new morality of Christ and face every situation under the compulsion of the highest demands of Christian love. This will apply to race, to war, to sex, to business, and to decision-making in personal and social living.

When our children were small we sought to teach them the meaning of the Ten Commandments as the great moral and ethical principles of life. They knew that moving traffic demands rules, or death and injury result: there are rules for skiing, rules for driving, rules for flying. When in the growing lives of our children, they came up against a particular issue of moral necessity, we did not always say, "Do it! You have got to! It's right!" We entered into a moral and spiritual struggle with them; we tried to help them think it through and see for themselves why it was right. We tried to help them discover why the moral principle made sense as the highest confirmation of this particular situation. After sweating through many moral crises with them and sharing their agony, we observed them discovering an understanding of high ethical principles, from their own insights as directives for great joy, freedom, and great living!

Our children have not been adequately instructed in moral and ethical living just by demanding that they memorize the Ten Commandments, alone. Our teaching is not complete until we have helped them understand and desire for the right reasons, to face their own particular life situations under the direction of these moral principles, interpreted by the highest demands of Christian love. As someone has put it: "Faith, hope, love, all are needed in the discovery of the *Responsible Self.*"

Obviously you do not tell the insane murderer where the hiding victim is. To protect a life you would lie. But the principle of truth stands forever as a valid principle of life! In the application of Christian love to difficult life situations, one does not make snap judgments; we struggle and sweat; we seek to understand justice in the situation: What does Christ-like love demand? What does the supreme will of God indicate? Prayerfully, one seeks deep insight. In faith, we seek to be wise, as Jesus was. We yield to that which we must under the imperative of Christian love. We are obedient to the clear demands of Christian integrity. Joseph Fletcher quotes Paul's statement in Philippians: "I pray that your love may abound yet more and more in knowledge and in all judgments."

The Christian accepts the highest level of moral and ethical demands and helps others to do so. Christian love is hard on sin, personal sin and social sin, because sin destroys life and relationships. Christian love is not permissive. Because of our permissiveness, many of our homes are producing more and more youth who are growing up unfit to make good homes for their children, who will in turn grow up unfit to make good homes for their children. A police officer told me recently that he had to call three parents and tell them that their sons had been arrested on drug violations. He received the following replies: 1) "Not my son!" 2) "Tell me what to do." 3) Just sob after sob!

Dr. Menninger, one of our great psychiatrists, says, "Conscience develops in the early years, and we have to work at it." We do this by working through situations with our growing children until they discover in their own minds the desire for high moral life, because God, our Father, requires it. As we look at our own children we must remember: Even a Steinway needs tuning.

Christian love is never self-centered ethics; it is God-centered ethics, love-centered ethics. A recent book, *Integrity Therapy*, reveals that psychiatry is beginning to understand the relationship between high moral commitment and mental health. When we begin to understand how much God cares for us, we seek to obey his inner guidance. This is the radio beam of human relationships. This is the basis of our hope for an ordered society. There are things we do not have to tolerate in the name of tolerance!

At this moment there may be some young man, or young woman, somewhere in the world, crushed by the awful consequences of permissiveness, who stumbles blindly into some unknown sanctuary, falls on his face before the altar, trembling, feels the presence of God's Power, perceives an inner light within his mind, and catches a vision of God's righteousness and love.

He sees God and humanity and person to person in new eternal relationship. He sees it as it really is! He rises to walk back into the world to share the vision. And humanity will once more, through the radiance of his face, be excited into new commitment and respond to God's call to the highest possible life, under the guidance and power of God's love and righteousness, and the Eternal Kingdom will draw a little nearer.

The Ten Commandments are God's yet unrealized, new morality, now realized in the dawn of Christ-like love. This is the runway. Put your life down here, and live.

Chapter 2

The Sea
Around Us

Listen, this is the whole universe speaking. More than the universe — the mystery at the heart of and beyond the universe. This is the ultimate word — the word of truth. God does have a word. It is written in the history of the universe; it is written in the mind and heart of humanity. It is recorded in the Bible, and partially recorded in the other great religions of the world.

God speaks, and we must listen. He says, "No!" in the Ten Commandments; he whispers, "Yes!" in the Beatitudes of Jesus. There are things we cannot do, because they upset all meaningful human relations. There is a spirit of life we should follow because this is the spirit of love and worship and human helpfulness that keeps humanity moving upward, joyfully.

But you say, "Nobody! Nobody has the right to tell me what I cannot do." But, yes! The Creator and Sustainer of the whole universe does. And he speaks clearly of guidelines that hold us back from self-destruction. You don't have to land your airplane on the runway. You can fly over it, short of it, or on either side of it — yes! But you are dead. God provides a runway where we may land and stay alive. It is mapped for us in the Ten Commandments. O God, keep me safely on the beam!

God caps off the route with the "Do's" in the Beatitudes of Jesus. If we have eyes to see, we are on the eternal road to life.

As Moses led the Hebrews from their slave drivers in Egypt, God knew that they could not now survive as a free people without the inner guidance and controls of a deep moral order, so he gave the Ten Commandments as the basis of high moral principles that must be followed. These principles were not just for the Hebrews, but for the whole human family. "No! There are certain things you cannot do and survive." And God means what he says.

There is an old, old story. The old snake had just swallowed a baby rabbit before he started through a small hole in the fence. He had thoughtlessly swallowed up another baby rabbit on the other side of the fence. When he pulled up to the first baby rabbit (like an orange in a Christmas stocking), he was stuck. And when he tried to back out, the second baby rabbit kept him from backing out. He was stuck, and the farmer came with a pitchfork to end it all. The snake's last thoughts were: "Here I lie, the victim of circumstances beyond my control." But, wait! He did not have to swallow the first rabbit. He did not have to swallow the second rabbit. After breaking the law of survival, he was helpless — he was dead.

In our understanding of life's directives we begin with the First Commandment: "Thou shalt have no other Gods before me" (Exodus 20:3). No! No other God but the One God who is at the center of life. He is the Creator, by the fact of creation, and has claim on the created. Humankind may reject him, but still he is Master! With our modern views of creation, we tend to forget that God is still at the center: the God who created atoms and breathed energy into the nucleus of the atom; the God who gathered these atoms into molecules and fashioned the universe; the God who flung the earth from the sun and set it in its proper orbit; who in one great moving tide of the semi-molten surface of the Earth scooped out the moon and flung it into space; who cooled this planet with his breath, and with stress and strain lifted up its mountains and sank its ocean beds; who made his steaming rains to fall and fill the seas; who created protoplasmic life within the waters of these seas; who developed that life, step by step, in the growth of complex, complicated forms of his own diverse and intricate design; who finally out of all of this, and by his wish, peopled the land, creating man in his own image — a living being, akin to God! This, our God, has a right to speak!

Einstein reminded us of our present, dangerous imbalance by saying: "We are living in an age of perfect means and confused ends." A new loyalty to God, the Creator, the Beginning and the

End of things, will clarify our ends, and thus direct our means to these ends; and man will be able to arrest his destructive sabotaging of the creation.

In him we live and move and have our being. He is the "Sea around us." Rufus Jones tells of a Sunday school teacher who started a Sunday school on a small fishing island off the coast of Maine. The island was so small that the ocean could be seen from any point on it. The waves could be heard throughout its length and breadth. The children went to sleep and waked by the rhythmic beat of its waves and tides. Most of their food came from the sea. They breathed the air from sea; the bathed in the sea and rode their fathers' fishing boats on the sea. The Sunday school teacher asked: "Everyone of you who has seen the Atlantic Ocean raise your hand." And not a single hand was raised. No one had told them its name. No one had identified for them the total environment in which they lived.

Dr. Jones continues to give us a glimpse of this "Sea around us": "We lie open on one side of our nature to God, who is the over-soul of our souls, the over-mind of our mind, the over-person of our personal selves ... there are spiritual hungers, longings, yearnings, passions, which find no explanation in terms of our physical inheritance or of our outside world." These answers are found in the enveloping "Seas of God" — God, our Heavenly Father.

In glorifying the process of humanity, we are apt to overlook one important fact. According to a fable, an angel spoke to the Devil saying: "We are in an age of evolution and you are doomed." To which the Devil responded: "Ah! but I too am evolving!" It is becoming clear that evolving man, by himself, is not outrunning the evolving focus of Evil.

Some time ago I was reminded by Harry Golden, an outstanding Jewish author, that when the Temple in Jerusalem was destroyed the Jewish father became the priest, and the Jewish worship was celebrated in the home. Each Jewish father taught his son to be the priest of the family, and that son taught his son to serve as the priest of his family. Perhaps this is the power that explains the unity of the Jewish race as it has undergone persecution and has

17

been scattered to the ends of the earth. God was kept as the central reality in the family.

My son revealed to me recently that he had learned to pray at our breakfast table. Then I remembered joyfully that every single day throughout his boyhood and young manhood in family prayer we had discussed with God the immediate interests of our family, and the important affairs of life around us. My son had become aware of the presence of God in his own experience. The "Sea" to him had become real and he had identified it. When Jacob wrestled with the Spirit all night long, he knew Who it was he wrestled with: Abraham had told Isaac and Isaac had told Jacob. At times our youth are wrestling with life, and know not that it is God they wrestle with.

It is stupid to say that "It doesn't matter what we believe, just so we believe." In his quest for truth and meaning, Buddha went into a long trance. When he showed signs of coming out of the trance, his disciples gathered close around to hear the revealed truth. The Buddha roused, but just sat and sat: No word at all. His silence was his answer! There was no answer! There is nothing. *Unlife* is the answer! Jesus, on the other hand, came praying, healing, teaching, forgiving, loving, and lifting people into "newness of life," and he said: "Follow me! My father worketh hitherto, and I work." "The work that I do ye shall do also." "Come unto me all ye that labor and are heavy laden." "Your Heavenly Father knoweth that ye have need of these things." "I have come that ye might have life and that ye might have it more completely." He backed it up with the crucifixion. He branded it upon the memory of humanity in the resurrection. In him we see revealed the name and the nature of the "Sea around us."

God works with persons and through persons to persons. He seeks to make himself real to each of us. He calls persons to do strange things and backs them up. I talked with a plastic surgeon from Chicago who had become disillusioned with lucrative practice in the city and had answered the call to Medical Missions in Pakistan. There, practicing his skills where the need was so desperately great, he found new joy, and said: " 'For me to live is Christ.' This I do from dawn till dark, and I love it — I love it!"

18

The Christian is one who does things that would never occur to him if he were not in touch with Christ.

Moral weightlessness does not work. The pulls and the demands of responsible living, the pulls and the demands of God's love upon us are necessary to health. Scientists are even telling us that weightlessness in space causes the heart and blood vessels to let down, causes the bone cells to deteriorate and muscles to sag, and that prolonged weightlessness could be dangerous. Moral and spiritual gravity generated by the will of God act inevitably in the affairs of men. A wise old African in an village of South Africa, crushed by abuse and evil leadership, said it beautifully: "But people who err against human life, like our chief and the white man, do so because they are more blind than others to *the mystery of life.* Sometime life will catch up with them and put them away for good, or change them."

The implosion of all the affairs and suffering of the world, crowding in upon our awareness through modern communication media, sets up an inner stress too great for us; the breakup of the Soviet Union, violence in South Africa, violence in America, the uncertain Arab situation, family and personal fears and burdens, all together, are more than we can absorb unless we are aware of the supporting "Sea around us," and can cry out with the Psalmist: "If I ascend to the heavens, thou are there, if I make my bed in hell, behold thou are there … even there thy hand will guide me and thy right hand uphold me." The "leukemia" of our unfaith is healed by yielding "our whole nerve center to Christ." By faith we know that, no matter what happens, nothing can ultimately harm us or our loved ones, and we are assured that life and meaning and the essential values will endure. Because God is God!

Bishop Kenneth Goodson of the United Methodist Church tells of flying into Birmingham, Alabama, at night. The pilot invited him into the cockpit to see the lights of the city. The Bishop said, "I don't see the lights." The pilot answered, "Look, over there against the dark." Again the Bishop asked, "Where?" The pilot answered, "It's against the dark!" Then the Bishop saw against the blackness the emerging glow of the city. The words of John welled up within him. "And I, John, saw the Holy City coming down from God out of Heaven." The Bishop continued, "I saw the Holy City emerging out of darkness because God had revealed himself to his people, and the people had discovered God, and they *cared*!" He continued, "Hallelujah! The Lord God Omnipotent reigneth." And "He is making all things new!"

"The sea around us" is sufficient! And we know its name! "Thou shall have no other Gods before me! For there is no other God!

Chapter 3

False Gods
And False People

We become what we worship! Paul Scherer warns us: "The drift in human history is never away from religion itself, but only a religion with God at the heart of it toward a religion without any God at all except of our own making. The central problem is not Godlessness. It never is. The central problem is always idolatry." Millions are caught in this trap, worshiping, obeying something other than God.

This brings us to the Second Commandment: "Thou shalt not make unto thee any graven image, or any likeness of anything that is in heaven above, or that is in the earth beneath, or that is in the waters under the earth: Thou shalt not bow down thyself to them, nor serve them" (Exodus 20:4-5).

Some time ago I had the privilege of hearing Captain Alan Bean of Apollo 12, one of the four men who walked on the moon up until that time. When someone asked him what he thought about in the critical situations of docking and landing, he answered that he had no time to think at all; he was busy following almost automatically the practiced procedures that had been worked into his subconscious mind over months of training. Bean was living out his commitments.

Walking successfully for a lifetime on the earth also required deep commitments. Moses realized that before his people could march farther into history they must be prepared for its pressures, its demands, and its crises. Some practiced procedures had to be worked into their subconscious minds. There needed to be an accepted way of life. Some things had to be settled: "To whom do we belong? To what are we committed? What are the guideposts that we are to follow?"

The situation at the foot of Mount Sinai was a tragic one, even for the human race. Moses was overdue in his return from the mountain. The restless people crowded upon Aaron saying: "Up, make us gods which shall go before us. This Moses who led us out of the land of Egypt, we know not what has become of him." In other words, they were saying, "Quick! Give us something to worship! Something to tie to; something that *we can control*! This God of Moses has a mind of his own!" And Aaron, fearing that he could not control them, gave in to their desires, even when he knew that they were false. So he took their earrings, cast them into the form of a calf, finished it off with graving tools, and set it up to be worshiped. They offered sacrifices to it. "They ate and drank, and rose up to play, copying the immoral customs of their neighbors." A false god, creating a false people, living together in false relationships!

Moses returned, saw what they were doing, and cast the Ten Commandments to the ground, breaking them. He called Aaron to him, and Aaron answered: "They demanded that I give them gods; so I cast their earrings into the fire and 'this thing came out.'" How often have we cast false commitments into the fires of life, and "this thing came out"?

Immediately Moses came to grips with the situation: He ground up the Golden Calf, spread it on their drinking water, and made them drink it. He called on those who were on God's side to join him. There was civil war. Moses and God's side were victorious, and several thousand of the Hebrews lost their lives. This "False God" business is expensive!

The Children of Israel had been too quick to accept the practices of their immediate neighbors. We, too, tend to give ourselves to the "worship fad" of the moment. In our actions we are now substituting many things for God. Moses, in the Ten Commandments, was seeking to put life straight; to whom do we belong? What is life's commitment? The first four commandments are about our relationship to God: No other Gods! No substitutes for God! Respect for the name of God! Respect for the worship of God! The true God speaks a true word to his people and expects real obedience to his guidance.

Look at our world today. How we are responding! Desert Storm! The senate hearings on Judge Thomas! Mass murders! Broken homes! Drugs! The loss of political and corporate honesty! What God are we obeying?

T. S. Eliot condemns us:

> *Where is the wisdom we have lost in knowledge?*
> *Where is the knowledge we have lost in information?*
> *The cycles of Heaven in twenty centuries*
> *Bring us farther from **God** and nearer to the dust ...*
> *The Word of the Lord came unto me, saying:*
> *O miserable cities of designing men,*
> *O wretched generation of enlightened men,*
> *Betrayed in the mazes of your ingenuities ...*
> *The wind shall say: "Here were decent godless people:*
> *Their only monument the asphalt road*
> *And a thousand lost golf balls...."*
>
> (from "The Rock")

Now we must dare to look at our own contemporary apostasy. Recently I read the novel, *The Ice*, by Charbonneau. It reveals some of the present sins of corporate action. Kusie, the head of a major oil company, with his office in New York, is contemplating some difficulties he is having with his oil drilling in the Antarctic: He says to himself, "Nobody believes in God anymore. Law is good up to a point. When it stops being useful — it doesn't mean a diddly. Don't let it get in your way." Thus he instructs his Antarctic operation manager: "Do whatever's necessary! Whatever's necessary."

The manager of his illegal operation in the Antarctic goes back to the site. A conservation group is about to stumble on his illegal mining setup, where he has discovered a fabulously rich vein of uranium. His team withholds weather information from a helicopter pilot and he flies to his death. A lifesaving rope is cut and a great scientist almost freezes to death in the exposure. The manager himself tries to push a woman scientist into a crevice, but is attacked by her dog and falls to his own death. All this, only because the top man in New York "doesn't believe in God any more,"

23

and gives instructions: "Do whatever is necessary! Whatever is necessary!" This deadly attitude is all too prevalent in the corporate life of the world today. "*Profit* is God. Let the bones fall where they will." It is not like this when God is the recognized authority center.

William Golding's story, *The Spire,* has amazing insight. The old dean of the cathedral had one consuming passion, to build a 400-foot stone tower above his cathedral. He lived for this, and sacrificed everything and everybody for it. The spire became his *graven image.*

In the process a workman falls to his death from the towering scaffold. The old dean thinks: "I might add it to the cost."

The Master Builder, forced to build higher when he knew that the foundations and the pillars could not hold the weight, cried out: "Father, Father! For the love of God, let me go!" The Dean drove on toward his goal.

The services had to be moved from the nave into the chapel because of the danger. And later the services of worship had to be discontinued altogether. The dean's "confessor," who tried to help him see his blindness, was dismissed. The dean cut himself off from his people; he didn't have time for them. He whispered to himself, "I must put aside small things. If they are a part of the cost, why so be it!"

The old dean, standing on top of the 400-foot tower, standing there on the swaying spire at midnight, saw in the countryside surrounding him the fires that his people had built in devil worship because they had been denied the worship of God! As he felt the sway of the spire and heard the groaning of the overburdened structure and saw the bending of the pillars, he said: "Oh, the lessons I have learned!" But he had learned nothing, only to bend everything to his own idolatry.

The dean was thinking: "It was so simple! It was to be my work! I was chosen for it … A single green shoot at first, then clinging tendrils, then branches, then at last a riotous confusion." Haunted by the cost of his folly, "He shut his eyes, and recognized instantly the impossibility of prayer."

An awful weakness possessed him, but in his weakness he began to see the truth: "I thought I was doing a great work; and all I was doing was bringing ruin and breeding hate." He cried out: "I'm a building with a vast cellarage where the rats live." The dean's Christ could have stopped the hurting and brought the healing.

Again the dean whispers a glimpsed truth: "God? If I could go back I would take God as lying between people and to be found there." Not in spires, not in business, not in professional victories, not in stocks and bonds. God, revealed in people!

As the end closes in, the dean sighs: "And what is heaven to me unless I go in holding him by one hand and her by the other?" "I traded a stone hammer for four people." "Father Adam" leaning down close to the dying dean, "could hear nothing, but saw a tremor of the lips that might be interpreted as a cry of: God! God! God!" So we leave the dean exactly where you and I must someday be left — with the wisdom and the Mercy of God, our Father!

God commands! He does not compel! This is the mandate of creation, the ground of our *freedom*, the *necessity* of our *choosing*! As we gaze into the depths of our own souls and gaze upon our vacillating loyalties and our unclear commitments, we know we cannot hold on to opposites. Some things exclude other things. The Golden Calf excludes the God of Moses. The "spire" excludes the people. Choose; we have to! Shall it be our own "graven image" (money, power, pleasure)? Or shall it be the God of Jesus? The old dean could bear witness to the fact that the agony and the hell of breaking with the false God and yielding to the true God is eternally worth far more than it costs!

"Thou shalt not make unto thee any graven images ... Thou shalt not bow down thyself to them, nor serve them."

Chapter 4

The Rediscovery
Of Reverence

To take life and the whole universe seriously is not to bring fear and sadness, but to experience stability and joy. This is finding one's own deep center and finding the deep center at the heart of the universe and letting the two come together in effective living. The Third Commandment speaks to this: "Thou shalt not take the name of the Lord thy God in vain: for the Lord will not hold him guiltless that taketh His name in vain" (Exodus 20:7).

The Third Commandment reminds us of the evils of profanity. When our language becomes careless, our living becomes careless. The language of the streets has slipped into our living rooms. And when we lose respect for God, we lose respect for each other. Not so with Little Anna, the little child adopted at age three off the streets of London whose story is told in the book *Mr. God, This is Anna.* When asked what she knew about God, she replied, "I know to love Mr. God, and to love people and cats and dogs and spiders and flowers and trees — with all of me." Later she said: "Mr. God ain't like us: we are a little bit like Mr. God, but not much yet." Anna had the insights of Christ. Our careless attitudes toward God today frighten me.

If we kept a tape of our conversations during a day and played them back at night, we might be amazed. When Jesus said, "Let your communication be yea, yea, and nay, nay," he was pointing out the importance of direct, simple, honest, meaningful speech. Careless speech indicates a deeper sickness. We are not taking life seriously because we are not taking the Center of Life seriously. We are thinking and speaking flippantly relative to everything, even to God himself. As William Gaddis puts it, "We are living in an age of publicity and duplicity in which the phonies have inherited the earth."

When we go to sleep at night we are helpless; anything can happen. It is good to know that our Heavenly Father watches over us — that he really does.

There is the touching story of Red Feather, an Indian boy. Before he became a man it was time for his ultimate testing. The chief and the boy's father led Red Feather deep into the forest at dusk. They left him in a small clearing where he must stay alone until daybreak. That night he heard all kinds of threatening noises, saw all kinds of bulging shadows, and trembled bravely through until sunrise. Then he caught his breath as he saw the tip of a bow barely visible from behind a tree. Suddenly his father stepped out telling him that he had watched over him all night long. It was then that Red Feather caught a glimpse of an Eternal Heavenly Father ever watching over his children with protective love and care.

Helen Joseph, in a little poem, speaks of a woman who was always behind a mask: "She had no face. She had become merely a hand holding a mask with grace." When we refuse to take reality seriously, we condemn ourselves to an aloneness in a universe where we cannot afford to be alone. When we deal with God honestly, it is more than just a feeling; it is a Christian response to life — to match my "intentionality with God's intentionality," my acts with God's acts. As Albert Schweitzer put it, "The love of God demands from all that they should sacrifice a portion of their own lives for others." Jesus put it: "Not those that say, 'Lord, Lord!' but those that do the works of my Father in heaven."

Plato used the analogy of a magic ring that would make its wearer invisible at will, so that he could do anything he wished without being seen. We do not have that ring, but the anonymity of urban life today, where persons feel that they are hidden, that nobody knows and nobody cares, is resulting in our moral breakdown. A rediscovery of the reality of God, that he knows and that he cares, can bring once more to us, even in crowded conditions of life, meaningful and effective living. It was the God of Christ that

Albert Schweitzer took with all seriousness, saying: "I went to Africa in obedience to Christ."

The Prodigal Son did not take his father seriously until he was hungry; then he went home and truly saw his father for the first time. A successful businessman told me: "We are too rich to be hungry. We can buy anything we want; we don't enjoy it. We can go anywhere or do anything, but it's no fun any more. What we need is a real depression." I responded that I thought he was wrong, and what we needed was not a depression but a new awareness of Christ, which would bring us to a voluntary self-discipline in the midst of our affluence, which would cause us to use our wealth, our strength, and our creativity for the sake of others and for Christ's sake. Then in the midst of a dedicated affluence, appetite and joy would return.

Refusing to take God seriously, refusing to react to life with meaning, is the kind of flippancy which would cause a person to walk up to the edge of the Grand Canyon for the first time and remark: "What a wonderful place to throw old razor blades." We are talking about the God of Abraham, the God of Moses, the God of Christ, and also the God of the astronauts. Gordon Cooper and Pete Conrad, looking back upon our planet from outer space, whispered reverently, "So vast, so beautiful, so overpowering." A Cosmic God whose nature is Christ, who takes the universe with seriousness, deserves to be taken with utter seriousness by us.

"Thou shalt not take the name of the Lord thy God in vain," because he is God, and because he seeks to bring each person and all humanity to the highest expression of life. He is the God who suffers with us and who loves us. He is the God who is deep in the subconscious mind (our subconscious mind), even deeper than the explosive confusion of neurotic and psychotic emotions; the God who can forgive and heal; who can control the passions and bring order to the chaos of broken personality. He is the One who is always standing in the shadow keeping watch! "He that keepeth Israel shall neither slumber nor sleep!" When I take his name in vain, he does not call down fire upon me. I do not destroy God; I lose my roots in life, and appetite and joy passes me by. I have lost my anchor.

Paul speaks of those who refuse to take God seriously, saying: "They seem to be all wrapped up in their own affairs, and do not really care for the business of Christ." This is our sin — all wrapped up in our own affairs, carelessly taking God's name in vain. Have we forgotten how Jesus closed the Lord's Prayer, "For Thine is the Kingdom, and the Power, and the Glory, forever"?

We seem to be unaware of the constant pull of the Spirit of God upon our lives. For a long time we have been aware of the tides in the oceans. Only recently have the scientists revealed to us the tides in the land — that twice a day, by the pull of the sun on the surface of the earth, the ground is lifted an average of twelve inches. Thus, invisibly God pulls each of us toward the fullness of life, and by the touch of Christ upon us, we respond.

The second part of this commandment, "The Lord will not hold him guiltless that taketh His name in vain," does not mean that God is mad at us. It simply means that we have cut the channels of our forgiveness because we are not accepting God's forgiveness as reality, and we cannot realize our forgiveness, but stumble on, heavy with guilt. A Godless world is a guilt-possessed world. A practicing atheist is one who has to carry his own guilt, because he has no place to lay it down.

When God is rediscovered, when Christ is rediscovered, we know inwardly that "the love and forgiveness of God are available to all persons, at all times, in all places." When love and forgiveness are rediscovered as reality, no longer are we the hopeless victims of our moods and our guilt.

To take God's name in vain is like the sailor laughing at the North Star, like the pilot of a passenger plane disregarding the radio beam, like the captain of an ocean liner closing his eyes to the compass: they are all on a collision course. To take God's name in vain is to miss the cosmic directive in life, and we are lost. To rediscover "The Master of the Universe" and to come with complete dedication under the Spirit of Christ is to know with assurance "that if I slip, Thou does not fall." This is the Gospel of Hope: it's the message of reality!

Christ took the Father with ultimate, ultimate seriousness and joy. He prayed, "Our Father who art in Heaven, hallowed be Thy name! Thy Kingdom come; Thy will be done on earth as it is in Heaven."

Christ, in reverence, is still the valid center of our daily living, and our Eternal Hope.

Chapter 5

Touching Base With God —
The Rediscovery of Worship

God commands that we give one day in seven to him. Worship is not a waste of time. It is the quest of life's wholeness; the discovery of meaning; the realization of hope! With the walls of our prisons closing in upon us, the ceilings of our lives dropping lower and lower, we are desperate and have no place to flee. We are mounted on a bigger horse than we can handle; the bridle is broken. The necessity of worship is obvious. For worship that programs faith into our computer minds is an available force that we must deal with.

The Fourth Commandment is very clear: "Remember the sabbath day to keep it holy. Six days thou shalt labor and do all thy work: But the seventh day is the sabbath of the Lord thy God: in it thou shalt not do any work, thou, nor thy son, nor thy daughter, thy manservant, nor thy maidservant" (Exodus 20:8-10).

A *New York Times* review of *The Divided Self* by R. D. Laing revealed the following about a central character: Julie feels crushed, smothered, flooded, burned up every moment of her life by terrible forces that never leave her in peace ... the most ordinary circumstances of life constitute a mortal threat to her being. She feels that she isn't a real person ... terrifying messages explode inside her: she was born under a "black sun"; she is a "prairie," a "ruined city," a "broken pitcher," a "well run dry," she is "the ghost of the weed garden." Julie is "a false-self system." Few of us are as bad off as Julie, but we are threatened with her symptoms — we are broken, scared, divided. This condition brings us face-to-face with the Fourth Commandment: "Remember the sabbath day to keep it holy." Jesus added another insight: "The sabbath was made for man and not man for the sabbath."

In a threatened, broken world, God seeks to give us wholeness, but what we do not have time for, we do not have. Many people are worship "dropouts." So life begins its steady deterioration, and humanity approaches the brink of nervous breakdown. Worship is like eating; it has to be practiced regularly if life and health are to be sustained.

William Golding, in *Free Fall*, suggests that we may "see the connection between the little boy, clear as spring water, and the man who became a stagnant pool." Golding describes the thinking of that little boy: "What should I do next? The graveled paths of the park radiated from me: and all at once I was overcome by a new knowledge. I could take whichever I would of these paths … I danced down one for joy … I was free! I had chosen. How did I lose my freedom? What was the decision, made freely, that cost me my freedom?" I believe that all of this has something to do with the lost art of worship. "Remember the sabbath day!"

We are constantly at the center of a thousand paths that lead outward. We have to take one, and that makes the difference. Life is an endless succession of intersections and choices. It is like paddling a canoe up a strange river — which of a thousand tributaries leads to the source? The wisdom and the love of Christ well up through 2,000 years of sabbaths and instruct us in our decision-making and walk with us down our chosen paths. In this is sanity and community, hope and eternal life.

We do not have to be a "broken pitcher," a "well run dry," or the "ghost in the weed garden" of a "ruined city." Some paths lead to great fulfillment and great meaning. Christ seeks to help us find these paths. He is a Living Presence realized in worship. "Remember the sabbath day" — the place of encounter and vision; the place of direction and strength and courage; the place of "marching orders" and the strength to see it through.

Once I stood at sunset in an ancient cemetery on top of a little mountain. A young man had just been laid to rest, and his little family had gathered around him in silence. During the prayer, I heard the soft lowing of the cows in the valley, the music of the cow bells in the distance, the living sounds that rose from the village. I opened my eyes to glimpse the vision: the river below, the green pastures, the homes, the little church in the center. I sensed God and peace. I was aware of meaning and of the Eternal. I was breathed upon by life and beauty! I was deeply aware of something; the bereaved family was aware of something — something that skiing and boating and outdoor weekends could never have told them. And then I remembered the description of a little village in Sussex, England: "When the lights twinkled in the windows on a winter's night, those straggly streets might seem like any other town, but it was not so; the church had touched the town." And Christ has met them there.

It was about thirty years ago that the shopping centers and the supermarkets struck our town in western North Carolina. The spirit of the community has never been the same. The stores stayed open all day Sunday. People worked right through church time; people shopped right through church time. Soon people were working on their yard on Sunday, and soon on their houses. All kinds of things, once done during the week, began to be done on Sunday. There could be a connection that soon more families broke up; that more and more unwed mothers had babies; that there was more and more crime, and murders, even among youth; that family worship and church attendance has diminished; that dishonesty was increased in business and government. Take the joyful worship of God out of the center of community life and deterioration soon follows. "Remember the sabbath day."

True worship can keep us *tough-minded* and *tender-hearted*, at the same time. And this is a good balance. With all our violence and moral breakdown, we are told that we have a "people problem": our people are not prepared; not trained; not inwardly committed to measure up to the demands of present-day life. Our people are too confused; they do not know how to handle it. It isn't programmed into the computer system of their minds. Again, with no apology, we must *teach* moral and spiritual values in our schools and our homes. Only thus are our people prepared to handle day-by-day life. Serious worship and training on the sabbath is an important part of this. Lose the sabbath and you lose this directive force for sanity and for good.

Once I saw a common mushroom break through a solid asphalt pavement. How was it possible for such a soft, spongy bit of life to exert such power? Perhaps it was hydraulic pressure as the cells drank up moisture; perhaps it was the mysterious pressure of growing cells. At any rate, the frail mushroom won its freedom. Genuine worship can bring such freedom to a confused, inadequate people, not prepared for life. Can this vital spiritual force enable them to break their false prison walls and push their way up to sane living and sane relationships? Yes! Because God, the greatest force in the universe, is back of it.

For centuries human beings have broken out again and again from pressures that have enslaved them. People have been made adequate and sustained to meet all kinds of crises. The moral righteousness of God, when accepted, gives strange power. The Spirit of Christ, when obeyed, produces a beautiful wholeness of life. Then "problem people" become "new creatures," "power people." There is power in worship! The switch is turned on, faces light up, love is experienced, and humanity moves forward.

Once Paul was one of the problem people, but his mind was captured by the mind of Christ, and he confessed: "The life I now live, I live by faith." Rufus Jones speaks out of experience: "God is more in the mind of man than anywhere else in the universe." This is where God operates; this is where he enters life effectively. But, as the astronauts must be trained through long periods of concentrated effort to experience the glories of space and to survive, so must we and our children be trained through worship experience after worship experience to know the glorious possibilities of life in our time and to be prepared for the wonder of the Eternal.

Through the spiritual tides of worship we have become (as the mountain men sing in the Andes):

> Strong as the tree against the wind,
> Strong as the rock against the river,
> Strong as the mountain snow against the sun.

For the law of the sabbath is the keystone of the arch of public morals (and spiritual courage); take it away, and the fabric falls.

The Archbishop of Canterbury seems to agree:

> *To worship is to quicken the conscience by the holiness*
> *of God;*
> *To feed the mind with the Truth of God;*
> *To purge the imagination by the purity of God;*
> *To open the heart to the love of God;*
> *To devote the will to the purpose of God.*

It is said by those who know that a child can listen to a sea shell and hear the sounds of tides and ocean swell. And further it is said that persons can worship deep and hear the whispers of God. From altar stairs where prayers are made, strange echoes rise: the cry of need, the beating pulse of human hearts, the prayers of the martyrs, the longing of the saints! In animated stillness where the cross hangs low, the Master speaks: "Go, sin no more." "He that cometh unto me I will in no wise cast out." "Father, forgive!" Eternal sounds leap forth in time: the shout of the resurrection, the voice of God, the whisper of Christ, the Hallelujah Chorus, the tramp of feet toward the City of God!

This is how Arthur Clough found peace and direction in an earthquake world:

> *It fortifies my soul to know*
> *that, though I perish, Truth is so:*
> *That, howsoe'er I stray or range,*
> *Whate'er I do, Thou dost not change.*
> *I steadier step when I recall*
> *That, if I slip, Thou dost not fall.*

"The sabbath was made for man!" Still we stand at the center where the trails lead out in every direction. Still we paddle up the river seeking the tributary that leads to the source. The little boy, clear as spring water, does not have to become the stagnant pool. For we begin to see deeper than the sunrise, and more distant than the sunset. The well run dry and ghost in the weed garden are no longer a threat. We have found the answer.

"Remember the Sabbath Day!"
"O day of rest and gladness!"
The runway is made clear.

Chapter 6

The Christian Home — Our Hope For A New World

The greatest danger we face in America today is the collapse of the Christian home. The home is so crucial to life that God included it in the Ten Commandments. We are about to be convinced that only responsible parents make possible responsible children.

The Fifth Commandment and Paul's exhortation paint a clear picture, "Honor thy father and thy mother: that thy days may be long upon the land which the Lord thy God giveth thee" (Exodus 20:12). In Ephesians 6:4, Paul completes the covenant: "Fathers provoke not your children unto wrath, but bring them up in the nurture and admonition of the Lord." If this double admonition is obeyed, the home becomes the center of life where the meaning of life is revealed, where truth is taught, and where glimpses of reality break through that shape the personalities of the next generation. The home can save us or let us drift into spiritual collapse.

Rufus Jones wrote of his Aunt Peace: "I came to feel, little by little, that this remarkable woman was on the inside of most matters of religion and life, and she carried me forward by a kind of inward life." Aunt Peace had the secret that Paul was talking about. One of the secrets of my own moral and spiritual growth was that I was aware of the fact that my mother suffered when I did wrong — and so did God.

Dr. Bernard Harnik of Bucharest tells of visiting a nine-month-old baby in the hospital. He became aware that the child was dying. The doctors were also aware of approaching death. But no one knew why. During the night Dr. Harnik waked at 3 a.m. and the intuitive thought came to him that there was something wrong between the parents.

Dr. Harnik went back to the hospital the next morning and told them the feeling he had, that something was wrong between them. The husband replied, "The fault's mine. I am in love with my secretary." Harnik replied, "That is the problem; the child can feel this break between his parents." The father said, "I will rethink my problem." He was restored to his wife. The boy got well. The healing of the children comes through the healing of the parents. And this is one of the real problems with the home in America today.

Where is the growing edge of life? How do children learn? How do we become what we are? What are our children becoming now? When the secular home breaks down, is this the end of the home or a new beginning?

Truth is rarely assimilated in one huge "hunk." It comes more in flashes of understanding; in glimpses of reality which become bridgeheads of experience and lead to the next revelation. In the novel *Free Fall*, William Golding looks back through the life of Sammy Mountjoy all the way to the beginning, to see what made him. In this story we catch glimpses, or insights, which will enable us better to understand ourselves, and more effectively share with our children in the growth process.

Sammy never knew his father, and this left a terrifying, empty spot in his experience. He remembered his mother as a kind of "shadow" who showed him no affection. (And this is so often the pattern for producing babies today.) Upon the death of his mother, he was adopted by an Anglican rector who did not understand children and was totally preoccupied with other things.

There were two creative teachers in Sammy's early experience. One teacher, Miss Pringle, by her keen dramatization of the Bible, opened up to Sammy vivid experiences of reality. He began to understand how Moses walked with God; how Jacob caught a glimpse of the Everlasting. He even perceived something of the meaning of the love of God on the cross. But Miss Pringle hated children. She was frustrated; she purposefully embarrassed Sammy in front of the class; she blotted out his dawning vision. So Sammy turned God off, and slammed the door on Moses and Jacob and Christ.

The science teacher was an atheist but he loved children and respected them. He communicated a material world of fascinating relationships. For him the stars sang and the atoms danced in rhythm and the children caught glimpses of an exciting physical universe. At first Sammy, being very intelligent, disagreed with the shallow mechanical view of this teacher, and continued to glimpse the deeper truth back of it all. But he loved his science teacher and soon accepted totally his atheistic materialism.

In developing childhood there is the time of innocence — no commitment; the child just "is," but he is absorbing experiences; then, suddenly, invisible lines are drawn, and attitudes and emotions are developed. In relationship to his playmates, Johnny and Philip, Sammy began to be both responsible and irresponsible. He and Johnny got into trouble and learned by these experiences. Philip was more subtle and used Sammy, as he used the other children.

Sammy remembered that one of his early teachers refused to discipline him, and "let my guilt stay on my back." Father Anselm gave the children at the church some flashes of insight: "You cannot see it … children; but the Power that made the universe and holds you up, lives here … take with you the thought of that Power, uplifting, comforting, loving and punishing, a care for you that will not falter; an eye that never sleeps."

Sammy was tricked by Philip into violating the altar of the church. He was hit by the verger so hard that it sent him to the hospital. The verger, disturbed by the severity of the blow, came to ask his forgiveness, and Sammy thought, "As I saw the truth, the adult world had hit me good and proper for a deed that I knew, consciously, was daring and wrong." The child wondered why the man needed to be forgiven for doing his duty. There are strange springs of truth and insight that seem to well up almost automatically in the mind of a growing child — also springs of evil.

In this crisis in his life, Sammy realized "there is no point at which something has knocked on the door and taken possession of you; you possess yourself." That isn't enough; there is nothing to mark you out from the ants and the sparrows." Therefore, in his materialistic atheism, he did what he pleased; and this led to an illicit affair with a young girl which destroyed her life. He simply said to himself, "What I was, I had become."

Later, in a Nazi prison camp, in solitary confinement, in total darkness, under the threat of torture, he experienced almost total personal disintegration. At this point we are reminded of the contrast of what happened to Sammy in prison and what happened to Paul, and we wonder if our children have been deprived of that inner light that might some day lighten their hour of total darkness.

Sammy, upon being freed from the blackness of solitary confinement and allowed to walk across the prison courtyard in that sunlight, experienced a whole new world of meaning and aliveness and light exploding within his subconscious mind. He saw flashes of the ultimate and the everlasting. He was overwhelmed with just being alive! He cried out in joy, saying: "The cry was directed to a place I did not know existed, but which I had forgotten, merely; and once found, the place was always there, sometimes open and sometimes shut; the business of the universe proceeding there in its own mode, different and indescribable."

In our homes, in family prayer, in in-depth communications, have glimpses of the everlasting living reality been opened up to our children's awareness? Have we parents "gotten out of the way of that shining, singing cosmos, and let it shine and sing"? Sammy added with insight: "I don't believe, merely — I see." What if our children "never see"?

In his moral struggle, Sammy realized: "If a man is the highest, is his own creator, then good and evil are decided by the majority vote." "Our decisions are not logical, but emotional." "People are the walls of our rooms, not philosophies." It all turned out that Sammy ended up saying: "Why should not Sammy's good be what Sammy wants?" And then he declared: "Mine was an amoral, savage place in which man was trapped without hope, to enjoy what he could while it was going."

Without a loving God in our consciousness and in the growing awareness of our children, a lovely and fascinating universe is warped and spoiled, and we come out where Sammy did, hopeless and alone.

Seeing the girl whom he had once loved and destroyed, living now in total hopeless insanity in an institution, Sammy, with maturing insight, declared: "Cause and effect; the law of succession. Statistical probability. The moral order. Sin and remorse ... They are all true. Both worlds exist, side by side. They meet in me. We have to satisfy the examiners of both worlds at once." Then he added in desperation: "Both worlds are real. There is no bridge." But there is a bridge; and Sammy had begun to glimpse it. The bridge is in us, in God, in Christ; and it is real! The *authority* of parents must be "an experienced authority," where the light shines through and children "see" both worlds present at once.

Sammy, pulling himself out from under the rubble, realized himself late. The question is: Where? When? How do they *become*, these children of ours? Through what varied and interrelationship of experiences? The Christian home is a center of life where both worlds are known: It has the atmosphere of God, the climate of Christ, the good smell of faith, the air of goodness, the flow of understanding, and a sense of mission against the actuality of humanity in struggle. It is a safe place.

Christian parents *care* and their children know they care. I knew my mother suffered when I did wrong. I felt it, and it made a difference. Christian parents stand for something and their children know what they stand for. Christian parents believe in something great and their children know what they believe in. Christian parents *love* and their children *know* that they are loved — and they sense the fact that God loves. Christian parents demand much of their children and their children are glad to be challenged and pulled up on tiptoe. These parents are moved by the mystery of God and their children begin to find themselves living within the mystery of God.

God made all this clear when he gave us the Living Christ to live and walk among us. To borrow words from Samuel Miller: Thus our children "become bold enough to affirm God in the midst of temporal imperfections, and strong enough to follow Him in the pilgrimage of moving time." And like Rufus Jones, these children are "immersed in an environment of a religion of *experience* and reality." It is an insanity not to let our children in on the depths of eternal reality!

Glimpses of truth determine life! May we parents, therefore, in a new seriousness of purpose, become worthy of the honor, and in faith, expose these little people of the future to the "nurture and admonition of the Lord."

God save our homes!

Chapter 7

Reverence For Life —
Thou Shalt Not Kill

We are disobeying God. According to *Time* magazine, 1990 was "the deadliest year yet." The U.S. still leads the world in homicides: "roughly 25,000 in 1991." Yet the Sixth Commandment says: "Thou shalt not kill" (Exodus 20:13).

And how many did we kill in the Middle East in 1991? I am not proud of it. Reverence for life is crucial in man's relationship to man and in man's relationship to God. But life is cheap. It is easy for persons to kill persons. With all our enlightenment, there has been more killing in the twentieth century than in any other era of history. One of the reasons for this is that much of humanity has lost its God perspective. "Thou shalt not kill." "Who says so?" And we do as we please.

A few months ago when I was preaching in Charlotte, North Carolina, the moon passed between the earth and the sun. For a few moments our segment of the earth was in darkness. There was an eerie light, temperatures dropped, and dew formed on the grass. Animals were in confusion. But if you looked at the place where the sun was supposed to be, you saw the corona, the flare of the sun, shining all around the edges of the moon. Soon the moon passed on in its orbit and the sun broke forth in all its life-giving strength. Even in eclipse, the sun is the only source of the earth's life and energy.

We are living in an age when the Living God, involved in every facet of life, has been temporarily eclipsed. The clear light of vision has dimmed; there is fear and confusion everywhere; man cannot see his brother clearly. Even the temperature of human relations is low. But we look at the place where God had been, and where God still is, and we see the corona of his glory! Even in eclipse, God is the only hope of humanity's redemption and our ultimate fulfillment of life.

"Thou shalt not kill." "Who says so?" The God who has been eclipsed and is returning says so. Man will rediscover consciously and subconsciously his place and responsibility in relation to other persons, and in relation to the universe. He will realize once more that he is actually dependent upon the creator, that he is subject to the will of God.

There is much hope even in the temporary shadows of eclipse. Alan Walker, in *Breakthrough*, reminds us: "The history books of the future could easily label human attitudes to war, pre-Vietnam and post-Vietnam." At this moment in history the real ferment relative to war and peace has begun. Here the viability of war is questioned openly. Now the United Nations is becoming more effective and public opinion is beginning to be formed.

Even Dwight Eisenhower, our top general in World War II expresses a strange opinion: "Every gun that is made, every warship launched, every rocket fired, signifies in the final sense, a theft from those who hunger and are not fed, those who are cold and are not clothed."

Great souls are in struggle here. You see Albert Schweitzer on an African riverboat, head in his hands — three days he had been in deep concentration — "struggling to find the elementary and universal conception of the ethical. I was wandering about in a thicket in which no path was to be found. I was leaning with all my might against an iron door which would not yield ... late on the third day, at the very moment when, at sunset, we were making our way through a herd of hippopotamuses, there flashed upon my mind, unforeseen and unsought (that mystical insight that reaches deeper than logic — that human calculating machine which, if you feed it a problem and set all its energies upon it will feed back an answer — that voice of God in man's soul), the phrase, *reverence for life*. The iron door had yielded, the path in the thicket had become visible." God had spoken!

In Colin Norris' book, *A Humanist in Africa,* a Rhodesian black boy writes to the white Christian missionary: "I wish to consult you about my problem which is this: I am a Christian of a Christian family but also a Nationalist … I want to join the Freedom Fighters but my religion worries me. Can a Christian take up guns and sticks against his fellowman? I am afraid of God and my conscience and not of white soldiers. What if innocent people — women and children — get hurt in our battles? Is there any excuse?" One's view of God, one's view of Christ, are still basic in this matter of killing.

Killing is not only in war; there are many ways to kill. Frederick Durrenatt's story, "Traps," in a recent issue of *Together*, speaks to this: "It's dog-eat-dog in business, you know — an eye for an eye and a tooth for a tooth. If you handle people with kid gloves you get kicked in the guts for your pains. I'm raking in the dough nowadays, but I slave like ten elephants for it … I must admit I didn't play exactly fair when it comes to cutting old Gygax's throat, but I had to get on. No help for it. Business is business." If there is no God, if I determine values all by myself, why shouldn't I take my boss' wife, take his job, and drive him to suicide? But God will not stay in eclipse; he stands over against us!

"Thou shalt not kill." Thou shalt not cause others to die — thou shalt not allow others to die through your own carelessness! A child dies because of bad conditions in substandard rental property. Who is responsible? A youth, speeding at ninety miles an hour, rounds a curve and kills six innocent people. Who is responsible? A thoughtless young husband, through many minor cruelties, makes his wife so miserable that she takes an overdose of sleeping pills. Who is responsible? A high school boy insists that his date drink with him, and he takes advantage of her. Knowing that a child is coming, she takes her life. Who is responsible?

Two boys go into a store in our city and kill the grocer. At the same time, a man knocks down a courier in a parking lot, sits on him, and shoots point blank into his head. Our young men continue to kill and be killed in foreign conflicts. Two national white leaders and one national black leader are assassinated in a brief period of time. The abuse of drugs is taking thousands of lives. Young teenagers are killing each other on our streets and in our schools. America's murder rate surpasses all other nations (roughly

25,000 homicides in 1991). Listen! Let me tell you about this God who has been in eclipse — Let me tell it like it is! And was! And ever shall be!

This *reverence for life* is a demanding thing, but when taken seriously it is a healing force. "Reverence for life does not allow the scholar to live for his scholarship alone ... It does not permit the artist to exist only for his art ... It refuses to let the businessman to imagine that he fulfills all legitimate demands in the course of his business activities. It demands from all that they should sacrifice a portion of their own lives for others."[1] We are not living as Christians unless we do this. Christ expects that we love and serve each other.

In the dawn of time when man was a child, Cain hated Abel because Abel got in his way. Man-Cain killed Man-Abel, and that was that! No, that was not that! An uneclipsed God intervened. He stood over against Man-Cain and said: "Where is Abel, thy brother?" And Man-Cain answered: "I know not: Am I my brother's keeper?" Cain would have closed the case at this point, but Cain was not the "Master of the Universe," and strangely he knew it. So he listened when God spoke: "What hast thou done? The voice of thy brother's blood crieth unto me from the ground ... Now art thou cursed from the earth ... A fugitive and a vagabond shalt thou be" (Genesis 4:9-13). And Cain went forth from the presence of the Lord. And it was dark!

Now Man-Cain kept his "books in balance": an eye for an eye, a tooth for a tooth, a life for a life. The books were balanced by death. You hurt me; I hurt you; you hurt me again; I hurt you again — get even, get even, get even again; it all adds up to death. Man-Cain insisted on justice: A life for a life! The ethnic hatred and the ethnic killings all over the world bear witness to this ancient system. So the rhythm of death possessed humanity. The cycle of death mounted and mounted. God saw this and acted!

God broke in upon his fractured creation with Christ-man. "He came unto his own, and his own received him not." He loved — they hated. He healed — they hurt. He turned the other cheek — they struck him again and again. He went the second mile — they drove him to a cross. He said: "Father, forgive" — they drove the nails deeper. He died! He arose! He came back, loving and saving. He broke the cycle of hate and death! Christ-man is different from Man-Cain. Christ-man saves Man-Cain from himself.

Something has to give between Man-Cain and his brother; between Man-Cain and his wife; between Man-Cain and his child. Somebody has to break in with a different spirit. Sheer justice leads to death (an eye for an eye). Somebody has to take all the blame, for the moment, so that doors of reconciliation can be opened and then the other person can say: "It's my fault, too." Then the death rhythm is broken by forgiveness: the second mile! The other cheek! A cross! "Father, forgive." Now the cycle of *get even* is broken; humankind is freed to love, and peace is the climate of human relations.

The books are balanced by forgiveness. With Man-Cain God is in eclipse; with Christ-man God shines through. "Thou shalt not kill!" "Thou shalt love thine enemy!" Who says so? God says so on a cross! And in the words of Kenneth Kaunda, former president of Zambia: "We have moved on from the survival of the fittest to the survival of the Highest." We can follow a tough Christ, through tough choices, to a tough peace.

With Man-Cain, humanity is *murderer*; civilization is *killer*. With Christ-man, "We start building bridges, hoping that someone is building from the other side." Look at Russia and the United States. Under God, "Man belongs to man; man has claims on man."

"Am I my brother's keeper?" An uneclipsed God stands over against the world and says: "Thy brother's blood crieth unto me from the ground!" Man-Cain finally sees; he becomes Christ-man; Eternal life is born!

---

1. Albert Schweitzer quoted in *The World of Albert Schweitzer.*

Chapter 8

Man, Woman, And God —
Thou Shalt Not Commit Adultery

This is the origin of the human family, and God's command that it be protected. The Seventh Commandment has to do with life — its beginning and its development. This commandment might be stated: "Thou shalt preserve the richness of human love."

Where is the center of life? Most of us had no difficulty in recognizing this center at the heart of the home when we were children. There was warmth and light there. There was a father and a mother who loved each other deeply and who loved us. There was integrity, understanding, forgiveness, hope, and faith. To us this was the center of the universe, and it was good. We got the picture. We knew security, and we moved with hope toward the fulfillment of our lives. Now we ask ourselves: Where is the center of life for today's children? Do they know warmth and light, faith and hope, forgiveness and understanding? Do they see a warm affection between their parents? Do their parents obviously love each other?

Many children and youth today have no viable center of life. No joyful, loving father and mother. No meaningful picture of life and the universe. No security of hope. The center has collapsed and life has collapsed. This is why the Seventh Commandment demands that we shall do nothing that will destroy the rich meaning of human love, which is the viable center of life for the next generation. Thou shalt preserve the love and the trust that makes life warm and beautiful.

But when I look about me today, I am deeply frightened. In our newspaper, "Court: Daughters can sue father for rape damages." Parents are sexually abusing their children. How far we have drifted from an awareness of what God expects of us, and an obedience to it! The U.N. reports that 95 percent of Swedish girls have participated in sexual relations before age twenty; 66 percent of American girls; while only 17 percent of unmarried Japanese girls have experienced sex by that age. Has the world lost its guideposts? Have we surrendered the meaningful home of lasting love and trust? Are we willing to put up with the terrible suffering and lostness that exists in a society without obedience to values? Perhaps the real meaning of love is caring and physical love controlled by a deep and lasting spiritual love.

Richard Foster, in his book *Money, Sex, and Power,* brings us back in line once more. "Fidelity means directing genital sex into its God-given challenge in the covenant of marriage … Fidelity means an enduring commitment to the well-being and growth of each other … Fidelity means mutuality … Fidelity means honesty and transparency with each other … Fidelity means to explore the interior world of the spiritual life together."[1]

Foster continues: "Adultery is not acceptable in any form for those who are followers of Jesus Christ."[2] It is true that God made us "male and female" (Genesis 1:27). He made us man and woman intentionally. He created sex on purpose as one of the greatest life-enriching experiences. God also created or established the boundaries in which this marvelous experience could be consummated. Destroy those boundaries and you bring tragedy. Foster suggests: "Sex outside marriage is wrong because unmarried persons thereby engage in a life-uniting act without a life-uniting intent." The sex act indicates a deeper union — a uniting of heart, mind, soul, and spirit. That's where the lasting joy is.

But why do homes break down? Why do they run off the runway and crash? Some of the answers are: lack of commitment; lack of unselfish concern for each other; lack of joyful give and take; too little time for each other; too tired to express love; one or the other putting off responsibilities. The pressures of the modern world have a lot to do with it. They fail to realize what I heard in a recent sermon: "And God was there all the time." To realize this makes a difference. "Man, woman, and God" make a joyful combination. Leave out any one of the three, and it doesn't exist.

Our youth are getting a bad start. The music that they are devoted to, the television and movies that they watch, the books and magazines they read, the alcohol and drug culture surrounding them, the lack of high moral values in their schools, all of this does not point to the establishment of a wonderful, joyful, permanent home of love and values later on.

Carelessness now does not produce beauty and deep love later on. Two Wisconsin sociologists did a survey of 13,000 people who lived together before marriage. This survey testified to the fact that those living together before marriage were twice as likely to be divorced in ten years than those who did not live together before marriage. Promiscuity now does not produce faithfulness later on.

An abstinence program used in a California junior high school reports a reduction of pregnancies from 147 in the 1984-85 school year to only 20 in the 1986-87 school year. Something can be done about it! A study in *Christianity Today* suggests that the *Christian Church* must create a *sexual counterculture* over against the blatant sexual revolution of today. God backs this up; Christ backs this up. When we really throw ourselves into it and thus teach our children, we, under God, can change the picture. We must!

Recently I wrote a parody:

> *Our children hear our voices;*
> *We know them and understand them.*
> *They put their faith in us*
> *And follow us:*
> *By the help of God*
> *We lead them into life.*
>
> *They shall not be led astray*
> *Or lost;*
> *No man, no force*
> *Shall snatch them from us:*
> *For we give ourselves for our children.*

Our father who gave them to us
Is greater than all the powers of evil;
If once we lead them to Him,
No temptation can carry them away.

R.G.T.

A home where faith and love are real can bring a new age.

Desmond Morris, in *The Naked Ape*, sees the necessity of the *permanent* pairing of man and woman even from a biological point of view. He suggests, "The space ape still carries a picture of his wife and children with him in his wallet as he speeds toward the moon." Biologically, this is necessary because of the long period of training demanded by the human animal. It takes a permanent home to train a whole and balanced person. Jesus, seeing from the point of view of a loving Heavenly Father, adds: "For this cause a man shall leave father and mother and shall cleave to his wife: and the twain shall be one flesh ... what, therefore, God hath joined together, let not man put asunder" (Matthew 19:6). The *Interpreter's Bible* speaks of "a growing and eternal element in the love of a man and a woman ... in which both souls and bodies, the whole being, glow ... in mutual transfiguration." True love is fulfilled and developed in marriage throughout life.

Recently I noticed a two-page advertisement by AT&T. Steps were running up and down; one set of steps blue, another red, another orange, another purple. On these steps little men were rushing, up and down, up and down; but none of the steps converged and none of the men communicated. I felt that often this is the picture of a home that is not a home — husband and wife, children and parents, rushing up the steps and down the steps, day after day, and never really meeting, never communicating, never understanding; and the children are lost because the parents are lost. When a home is broken it is broken from the inside. Love is allowed to lapse and love dies. After this, neglected love is easily violated.

When love is real and the richness of growing love has been discovered; unfaithfulness is out of the question. Leigh Hunt says it for us:

For there are two heavens ...
Both made of love — one inconceivable
Ev'n by the other, so divine it is;
The other, far on this side of the stars,
By men called home, when some blest pair are met
As we are now ...

Husbands and wives, who have really discovered each other, live in a rich world. She is always there; he is always standing by; strength and joy are realized in each other. They realize that God has always been present in this experience of continued joy.

The Seventh Commandment points out the necessity for personal purity. There are six valid reasons for this. (These six reasons I borrow from a book I wrote on the home several years ago.)

1. "Animals can act like animals and be at peace. Not so with man." A human being has a mind, emotions, spirit, as well as body. Sex in marriage is an essential part of the development of understanding, love, and wholeness. It cannot be written off by either partner. But sex outside marriage can tear a person asunder. Once I received a phone call from a man from another city who, as a result of an affair outside of matrimony, was becoming the father of a child. The whole affair was about to break wide open, and he felt he was being forced into suicide. *When purity goes, the meaning of life goes!*

2. "Sexual irregularities defeat the highest purpose of life." It is impossible to build fire doors in personality and say, "I won't let this affect the rest of my life." Every triangle that I have observed has brought uncertainty, fear, and indecision into other areas of life of the persons involved. Inner conflict cannot be walled off. Sex is an act of total personality. Deep subconscious conflicts and disturbances arise from the neglect of faithfulness. *When purity goes, peace of mind goes.*

3. "Illicit relations are not just denying custom — they are breaking deep universal law." They are defying personal bonds of trust, and closing the doors of faith which life has built. When we fulfill the true relations of love, joy unfolds; when we defy them, the dark shadow closes in. It is against moral law, against the law

of God, against the law of love to tamper with loyalty and affection. We see the stupidity of the statement of an outstanding columnist: "Sex between 'consenting adults' is nobody's business." There are questions that must be asked: What about the wife of the "consenting adult" — her life, her feelings? What about the husband of the other "consenting adult" — his life, his feelings? What about the children of the "consenting adults"? What about the two centers of life, the two homes that are being violated? And more than this, what about "me," the "consenting adult"? What do I really want? What kind of person am I? What do I really want to give myself to? What about my present and my future as a self-respecting individual under God? *When purity goes, character goes!*

4. "Unfaithfulness harms those nearest and dearest to us." Birth control devices do not prevent the psychological death of trust and love violated. A whole person does not want to strain or hurt or harm anything so tender, so beautiful, as love realized. Infidelity puts out the light and leaves the home in darkness. We need each other — husband needs wife, wife needs husband, parents need children, children need parents. When we see it as it is, who wants to commit adultery? Who wants to destroy the trust of one with whom they have entered into the mystery of life? When one loves his family, loves his wife, and loves his children, peace is too deep, joy is too great, to throw away. *When purity goes, the home goes!*

5. "Man cannot long endure in an immoral society." Immoral man makes immoral society. There were many good homes in Rome just before its fall, but not enough of them to stabilize its life and prevent its fall. Any practice which endangers the next generation, which brings children into the world without provision for their care and guidance, is personally wrong. A strong civilization can never be founded upon moral laxness. *When purity goes, civilization goes!*

6. "God cannot be known with an impure heart." When we are defying love, when we are breaking with faith and trust, when we are destroying a loved one, we don't want to come into the presence of God. We run and hide because we are embarrassed by the light. In *immorality* we sever relations with *immortality*. When we

deny the will of God, we cannot know the peace of God. When we revolt against his laws, established for the preservation of the best in life, we cannot have the best in life. God is hard on us, because he loves us and wants the best for us. *When purity goes, the peace of God goes!*

To sum it up, immorality is a sixfold sin: against oneself, against life at its best, against those we love, against the next generation, against civilization, and against God. Blessed are those whose hearts are pure!

There is a straight runway for the home, and you can land there with safety. Man, woman, and God depend on each other.

How can the *Law of Love* be fulfilled? I am reminded of a story told by Harry Emerson Fosdick about a sixteen-year-old girl from California. The father had deserted the family; the mother had died suddenly and left this girl to care for seven younger children. She became a mother to them — kept them clean, fed them, and kept them in school. When she was praised by the neighbors for her faithfulness she answered: "I cannot take any credit for doing something I have to do." But they answered: "You don't have to." "Yes," she replied, "that's true, but what about the 'have to' inside me?" This is the secret — the "have to" inside us. The love of God constrains us; the love of husband or wife compels us; the love of children disciplines us; and we discover that the strength of a Christian home can weather the storms of a world gone mad. Christian love is that of two persons, each devoted to the fulfillment of the other, and thus, each being fulfilled, and fulfilling the lives of their children.

"Thou shalt not commit adultery." Thou shalt preserve the *center* of life. Thou shalt preserve the richness of true love. In the journey that we make together there is the threat of all kinds of difficulty; also there is the promise of fulfillment. Faith and love are on the side of the home's fulfillment. Let the life force work. Listen to the inner music. Attend to the beckoning of God. Grow in the richness of love. Let your children find their hope in the home — the eternal center of life!

───────────

1. Richard Foster, *Money, Sex, and Power* (Harper and Row), p. 151.

2. Foster, *op. cit.,* p. 161.

Chapter 9

Life Yields Only
To The Honest Man

The Eighth Commandment puts it to us directly: "Thou shalt not steal" (Exodus 20:15). The universe is built on the foundation of honest dealings. Thou shalt not take what is not yours. Thou shalt not withhold what belongs to someone else. Honesty is a solid stance for living; dishonesty is a disruption of human relations.

What is honesty? Tommy defined it simply when questioned by his teacher: "Tommy, what is a half?" He answered directly: "A half is when you cut something in two pieces and don't care which one the other fellow gets." We have laws to keep us honest; but laws cannot keep us honest. True honesty is enforced by character. Am I the kind of person who takes something that isn't mine? Or, am I the kind of person who cannot do this? We become honest or dishonest by commitment and by practice. It is a quality of life.

Dostoyevsky revealed how far we have drifted from a recognition of true character in his novel *The Idiot*. The Christ-figure Prince Myshkin was without greed, without malice, without envy, and without vanity. He was a beautiful person, but his contemporaries thought he was an idiot. They had lost the concept of character, and Russia collapsed. We are in danger.

The demon in the love of money is greed. We need to recognize a new call to obedience to Christ in relation to our use of money. We are shocked to realize how rich we are when we discover that if we own a house we are more wealthy than 95 percent of the people of the earth. Many people are even becoming psychotic over their relation to money. Dr. Karl Menninger tells of a wealthy patient who, when asked what he was going to do with all that money, replied, "I get such terror when I think of giving some of it away." He was hooked.

Richard Foster suggests a way we can take it with us. *People* will be in heaven. Give money to needy people and needy causes. Thus you can take it with you.

Foster outlines the Christian position in relation to business:

1. *We affirm the goodness and the necessity of work.*
2. *We affirm work that enhances human life and shun work that destroys human life.*
3. *We affirm human value above economic values.*
4. *We affirm the need to enter into each other's space in the employer-employee relationship.*
5. *We refuse to buy or sell things (harmful).*
6. *We refuse to take advantage of our neighbor.*[1]

Charles Kinsley suggests that there are three kinds of people: "First, the honest man who means to do right, and does it; second, the knave who means to do wrong, and does it; third, the fool, who means to do whichever of the two that is pleasanter at the moment." Perhaps the ones we need to guard against most are the fools — those of no character who can wreck any stable society. Character is that part of us that makes up our minds and holds us in line. When we do not respect the rights of others, interpersonal relations are thrown into chaos.

It is not sufficient to do business under legal specifications only. If deeper moral obligations are not recognized, we can easily find loopholes to escape the demands of honesty. When the ratio of honest men to dishonest men drops below a certain level, civilization crumbles. We may be dangerously near this point. Recently an attorney confessed, almost as if it were routine, to embezzling $100,000 in one year from his clients, and many corporations are allowing questionable practices in their business affairs. Even in a space age, civilization stands on the shoulders of honest men.

We smile when an individual in Malaysia is convicted for keeping $70 which was given him to bribe the police. In our own country, someone suggests, we might call a boy dishonest who steals a 25-cent bus ride, and look upon his father as "clever" when he, by a "smart" financial maneuver, steals the whole company.

Recently I read the life of John Tillett, an early Methodist circuit rider. His son, who was away at school, had endorsed for a friend a note for $85. The friend took off and left him with it. He wrote his father and his father answered: "Pay every dollar of it, if it takes you the rest of your life." The boy paid it. He became an outstanding attorney — he never forgot the value and integrity of a contract. This is how character is developed.

At this moment we might test ourselves, using some embarrassing questions worked out by Walter Duckat: "If after making a long distance call in a public booth, your money is accidentally returned, would you, or would you not, put the money back into the machine?" "If you were selling a house or a car with serious flaws, would you, or would you not, mention those flaws?" "If your car bumped another car and it was your fault, would you seek to blame the other driver?" "If you had a legitimate claim against an insurance company, would you pad it?" "Do you give your employer an honest day's work?" "What do you do when nobody is looking?" If we adults pass successfully these tests on inner honesty, it is likely that our children will appreciate an honest approach to life, and will be able to move out into a new generation on a more solid basis of human relationships.

Do you remember the cartoon where a man in a parking lot is seen to be writing a note and slipping it under the windshield wiper of a car whose fender he has just crushed? We read the note: "Dear Mr. Car Owner: These people watching me think I am writing my address, my license number, and my name on this card — they are wrong. Good luck!"

Now, what about our income tax? This is a tough one. It is a real test of integrity. We are told that the Internal Revenue Service received this letter: "Dear Sirs: Ten years ago I falsified my tax return, and since that day I have not been able to get a single good night's sleep. I am enclosing my check for $425. P.S. If I still can't sleep, I'll send the rest."

Thou shalt not take what thou hast not worked for! A stable economy is built on the foundation of every person producing something, creating something, or rendering some service, which he exchanges for a commodity, or a service, produced or rendered by someone else. When we take something for nothing by cheating, by gambling, or by stealing, someone else loses, and the economy is impoverished. The "sucker" isn't so much the man who is cheated, as it is the corner-cutting parasite who bleeds society white by taking out what he has not put in.

It is so easy to rationalize ourselves into dishonesty. Someone suggests this sequence of rationalization: "All men are good; some men are good. A few men are crooks; most men are crooks. All men are crooks — I had better get my share." When we judge ourselves against others rather than against God, we always end up at a lower level of personal character.

Thou shalt not withhold that which someone else has earned! An industry paying high dividends, and at the same time paying substandard wages, is dishonest — even if I am a stockholder. Someone suggests: "It is difficult for a poor person to withstand the temptation of taking that which does not belong to him; it is equally difficult for the rich person to withstand temptation to live a life of idleness." Either approach to life is dishonest. To have wealth is to assume responsibility for a segment of society! This is our stewardship.

God is still the Creator, the Owner, the Ruler, and he expects fair human relationships. Justice is simply the sophistication of honesty. It is dishonest to sit behind a desk, stand behind a counter, or run a machine, and not do our best; it is dishonest to employ a person to sit behind a desk, stand behind a counter, or run a machine, and not pay him a fair wage. An attitude of honesty and trust and a sense of fairness are essential to the continuation of our civilization.

The universe repudiates dishonest dealings. There is a God-force working within us to produce integrity and honesty. Man is honest when he seeks to discharge his duty to his wealth, to his ability, and to his responsibility. Thou shalt add to the enrichment of life! Thou shalt not scheme to take to thyself without rendering equal service to others. The Spirit of the Christian life is centered in "giving" and not in "taking." Our Master, Jesus, lived by this principle: "I came not to be ministered unto, but to minister."

In undermining a fair and just economic order, a man robs God. Life yields only to the honest man, and to him it yields abundantly. Paul put it briskly: "Provide things honest in the sight of all men."

Zacchaeus, the Jewish tax collector in Jericho, was caught in a web of unfair practices (of his own making). He was "marooned" on an island of dishonest dealings. He was caught up in this as a way of life; he had become this kind of person. His business was to take everything he could from his fellowman, in order to build up his own riches. Then to his amazement a luncheon engagement changed all of this, by changing him. In a new breakthrough of joyful honesty, because his outlook had been shockingly changed by a walk down the street with Jesus, he realized he had become a "giver" instead of a "taker." He could hardly restrain his joy.

"Thou shalt not steal." Thou shalt meaningfully preserve fairness and justice in all human relationships. And joy and peace invade the world.

---

1. Richard Foster, *op. cit.,* p. 70.

Chapter 10

Truth, The Only Foundation For Human Relations

We live by pictures — by the way we see life as a whole. William Golding wrote a fascinating story on prehistoric man, titled *The Inheritors*. It was set before the time of writing, when words were difficult and concepts were not clear. A member of the tribe would say, "I've got a picture": an event of the past; a situation of the moment; a glimpse into the future. The individual who had, or could describe, the truest pictures was the leader. Mal, the old leader, was dead. Ga, the promising leader, had disappeared. Fak, the next in line, was made the leader of the group. But Fak had difficulty with his pictures. His imagination was limited. He cried out under the weight of his leadership: "I wish I had many pictures, pictures that would follow one on the other." This problem isn't entirely prehistoric: As we struggle during an election year with the Democrats and the Republicans trying to gain the leadership of our nation, we yearn for a picture of a revitalized America. So many of us seem to have forgotten that this picture is realized only in relation to God and his vision for humanity. That is the *truth* we seek. If we are working for a safe, dynamic runway for life, this is the picture.

We have viewed Russia's fall from the *truth* while seeking the truth for their nation. We see them now rediscovering the truth in the rebuilding of their nation. As we see God being excluded from our own classrooms we see him being accepted once more in Russian schools. We are told that about 42,000 priests lost their lives in communist Russia, and 98 out of every 100 orthodox churches were "shattered." Now the picture is different. Even in 1983, Solzhenitsyn explained that the main cause of the disaster that happened to Russia was simply the fact that "men had forgotten God." Now many Russian leaders are admitting the same thing, that Russia had become "grievously starved for hope." The editor-in-chief of *Pravda* recently declared: "Morality is our worst crisis … and Christian values may be the only thing that will keep our country from falling apart." I believe that these values are the big picture for the world.

But at the moment America isn't doing so well with these Christian values. So much has been revealed of the dishonesty and breakdown of integrity in high government and industrial circles in recent months and years. We are in the same dilemma revealed in Job 28:

> *But where can wisdom be found?*
> *And where is the place of understanding?*
> *Man does not know its value,*
> *Nor is it found in the land of the living.*

In fact, it may happen as suggested in a recent novel: "Our people may some day die in the rubble of their wealth."

But there is another possible picture suggested by James S. Stewart of Scotland: "If we accept this Gospel as Christ's people, we will stumble on wonder upon wonder, and every wonder true." I like that kind of stumbling — stumbling upward!

The Ninth Commandment has much to do with all of this breakdown: "Thou shalt not bear false witness" (Exodus 20:16). That's where the integrity quotient breaks down. Today we need a true interpretation of life, based on reality, supported by fact. See it like it is; speak it as it is. Jesus said: "Let your conversation be 'yea, yea, and nay, nay,' " — simple, direct, and true!

Too many pictures thrust upon us today are not based on fact; do not give the basis on which individuals can make true judgments. Many pictures are to promote a product in order to sell it. This can be industrial propaganda, or political, or national, or personal. The promoters have their own "axe to grind." "Thou shalt not bear false witness" could be spoken to our advertising agencies. "The truth, the whole truth, and nothing but the truth," could bring us into focus once more.

This commandment speaks in an age of complex communication systems. What is the good of satellites, television, radio, or press that reach every little corner of the world almost instantaneously, unless we are broadcasting *truth*? Untruth, amplified on a world scale, is devastating. The Ninth Commandment is spoken to individuals, to groups, to nations, to all communications media: "Thou shalt not bear false witness." Hitler's Germany lived by a false picture and was destroyed by that false picture.

Jesus had a picture! A picture of humankind in true relationship with each other, under God! He declared, "I am the Truth." He added, "The truth shall make you free." One of our great problems is that we do not know the deep truth about each other, either on a personal or a national scale.

Pilate, in the presence of Jesus, asked a question: "What is truth?" Pilate knew pretty well what truth was. He knew it was wrong to crucify this innocent man. He was seeking to plead ignorance, and thus cover up his crime. The tactic is used by too many today. "What is truth?"

The Christian is one who has a clear picture; he is dedicated to the picture; he lives by the picture. He accepts the Kingdom of Christ's Spirit; his allegiance is to the kingdom of right human relations. If "truth is ever on the scaffold," it is because men love something more than they love truth. Many persons do prefer to live by falsehood. Conversion is rejection of falsehood and recovery of truth by the grace of God. Now we see it as it is; tell it as it is; live it as it is — "His truth endureth to all generations."

Lok, in William Golding's story, had almost no memory of the past, little vision of the future, and small understanding of the involvements of the present situation; yet, this simple prehistoric man was *true*. He told it like he saw it. He tried to see it straight. False witness was totally foreign to him. In our sophistication, we demand accuracy in space travel; we insist upon accuracy in medical care; we depend upon accuracy in our scientific and technological endeavors. Why then do we falter so in personal relations and in human relations? This is the recurring tragedy of history:

Human beings love something more than they love the Spirit of Truth. This is our downfall. It's a new contest every year, every month, every day … It's an enormous challenge to outwit one another as persons, as groups, as nations; and we become expert in bearing false witness. And Christ continues to beckon: "I am the way, the truth, and the life."

But in a recent cartoon, two exhausted little men appear on the blistered surface of the Earth. They whisper: "Our conquest of nature is complete — we have destroyed it." With Yeats we bemoan: "Things fall apart — the center cannot hold — mere anarchy is loosed upon the world." Both our ecology and our human relationships fail to measure up to the truth.

The Ninth Commandment emphasizes the devastation of false witness against one's neighbor: the tragedy of slander and gossip. Why do we speak untruth and imply untruth about other people? (The presidential campaigns are a sad example.) Is it that it makes us look good, or is it that it somehow relieves our own guilt or failure? Dr. Clovis Chappell says that you don't have to say it outright — just imply it: "Are John's accounts on the up and up?" "I am so sorry for Jim and Sue." Someone else uncovers the situation: "It isn't necessary that things be true, but that they have been said." Because of careless or malicious speech someone loses a job, or fails to get a job; friends are separated; homes are destroyed; lives are ruined. We back up white lies with gray lies, until the house of falsehood comes tumbling down on someone's head. Gossip and slander are stranger forms of recreation — or "reckeration." This commandment could be stated: "Thou shalt not deface; Thou shalt not undermine; Thou shalt not misrepresent." If we could only "paint the thing as we see it, for the God of things as they are."

According to Elton Trueblood, "Falsehood is an offense against the order of reality." A man living a lie is forever haunted by the truth. By the grace of God it is possible to match the truth of the universe with the truth of our living. We get at the root of things when we repudiate self-deception; then the *inscape* of our living comes into line with the *landscape* of reality.

Even our physical nature rebels against falsehood; the organs of our body rebel against untruth. This is the secret of the lie detector. Not even a seasoned criminal can lie without his blood pressure going up. We were created for *honesty* and *truthfulness*! Doctors tell us again and again that sickness easily invades a body that is living a lie. The Ninth Commandment underlines for modern man the basic importance of truth and integrity.

Truth in human relationships is *love*. The Christ Spirit is careful not to abuse "the naked truth," or to take advantage of "brutal truth." Christians "speak the truth in love." Some truths we should never repeat, unless it is necessary to save someone from deep hurt. Those who worship God, will worship him in spirit and in truth.

All truth is not clearly seen or understood; but to honest men truth is increasingly revealed. There is health and joy in observing truth; truth frees men from all kinds of hang-ups. The old South African tribesman, Dinorego, in the book, *Where Rain Clouds Gather,* concerned because men in his tribe defied the truth, said: "I think the Good God don't like it." But he said it as though "the Good God" was quite near, listening, observing. And he, Dinorego, was listening to the Good God. God is not coldly concerned with the truth; he has a warm personal concern for truth in relation to humanity.

We worship a God of Truth. Jesus came revealing truth. He gives it to us straight. The Christian seeks to reflect it straight. Grant us, Oh God, "truth in our inward parts." Give us the Spirit of Truth. "From cowardice that shrinks from new truth, from laziness that is content with half-truth, from arrogance that thinks it knows it all; Good God, deliver us."

"I've got a picture!" I glimpse the God of Truth. I glimpse a universe of truth. I glimpse man living according to truth. Here is the picture: "Man of truth, under the God of Truth, following the Christ of truth, walking in the way of truth!"

A Dutch sea captain had just saved the life of a young German seaman whose submarine had sunk the captain's vessel. The captain had thrown himself between the boy and the machine gun strafing of the lifeboat by a Nazi plane. The captain explains it:

"As I lay there, pressing his head against me, it was as if at the very last moment I had finally touched upon the sense of life, the meaning of it all, the essence of my existence. I had a feeling of such peace, such understanding, such serenity, that it came as an anticlimax, almost as a disappointment when the world fell silent, the roar of death drew away and I realized that I would have to go on living." The Dutch sea captain had the picture: Truth revealed in the life situation, in the face of life and of death — truth from God, experienced in a human situation.

"Thou shalt not bear false witness" in any situation. Thou shalt witness to the truth — the whole truth — in every situation. God is our Helper.

Chapter 11

Uncontrolled Desires
Will Wreck Your Life

I recall a cartoon in the *Saturday Review*: A corporate head is standing before the table at which the Board of Directors is seated. He states the situation: "Our days of gobbling up corporations are over. As of 10:15 this morning we've been gobbled up." Too often in the corporate world, we are either the grabber or the grabbee. That is not the way God planned it.

The Tenth Commandment speaks to a basic problem in human relationships and also to our own inner experience. It explores motivation. "Thou shalt not covet" (Exodus 20:17). Covetousness is to desire, ardently, especially what belongs to someone else. Jesus warns us: "Beware of covetousness; for a man's life consisteth not in the abundance of the things which he possesses." This final commandment is directed against selfishness and greed; it points us to generosity, concern and gracious living. It reminds us of our responsibility to "the least of these, our brothers." This commandment frees us from the limitations of selfishness, and brings us out into the rich life of love and caring.

Louis Charbonneau has one of his characters in *The Ice* say: "Nobody believes in God any more." And continues: "When (people) stop being useful to you, they don't mean diddly. Don't let them get in your way."[1] A great shadow has been cast over America and our way of reacting to each other. Greed has possessed us.

The novel continues: "He was trying to put a reasonable face on evil, Nately thought. It was the practical thing. It was necessary. It made possible a higher good. Perhaps men driven to embrace evil had always found a way to forgive themselves." But God doesn't forgive without genuine repentance — the universe is put together that way.

Maybe the answer to evil is spoken by a character in *Earthly Powers* by Anthony Burgess. Carlo was trying to protect a girl being tortured for information: "Carlo prayed aloud, but not for her. 'O merciful God, enlighten your three servants here, slaves to a diabolic faith. Drive out the evil from them, reinstate their lost humanity. Forgive them, they know not what they do.' "[2] You do not overcome greed with greed, nor do you overcome evil with evil. The spirit of Jesus can eradicate our greed and covetousness with his love and caring. Only this can heal.

Covetousness dictates to us. As Richard Foster says, "We must possess; we must hoard; we must conquer." And the world disintegrates in bitterness and death. Organized sin is powerful and all-consuming. Only the grace of God can empower us for the total renunciation of evil and its stranglehold upon us. But the ocean of darkness can be overcome by the ocean of light and life. Alexis Carrel states that under the power of Jesus' Spirit, "the world ceases to be cruel and unjust and becomes friendly, while a strange power develops in our own depths."

An outstanding national leader reminds our youth: "You can use your enormous privilege and opportunity to seek purely private pleasure and gain, but history will judge you — and as the years pass you will ultimately judge yourselves — on the extent to which you have used your gifts to heighten and enrich the lives of your fellowman." Many young people are beginning to repudiate a merely materialistic way of life. They have been articulate of late, and forceful, and yet most of their force and articulation has been *against* something. But in order to bridge the gap, the door is now open to discover the *creative values* that they do believe in, and to which they are willing to give their lives.

The real problem of our prosperity is not how to keep it, but how to use it. There has been a great deal of complaint against Big Business, Big Labor, and Big Government. Morris Blochman, quoted in a Dow Chemical Company advertisement, goes to the source of the problem, which is selfishness: "The most serious threats to individual freedom stem not from big business, big labor, big government, as they do from a business community primarily interested in acquiring large profits with little regard for the commonwealth; from a labor force primarily concerned with continually increasing its wages and job benefits — much like the profit motive of the businessman — with little or no concern for the welfare of the rest of society; from a government whose leaders are more concerned with justifying their policies and maintaining their power than they are with contributing to the solution of the problems of all the people." Selfishness and covetousness can destroy the good services of almost any segment of life. Selfishness is our problem. Covetousness is a poison that infiltrates all life's relationships.

J.S. Haldance wrote: "The universe is not only queerer than we imagine; it is queerer than we can imagine." It is hard to accept the fact that unselfishness is written into the constitution of things; that it is the core of good human relationships; that spiritually and subconsciously it brings the ultimate joy. My mother was an illustration of this. She always ate the "back of the chicken" until she honestly thought it was the "sweetest part." She sacrificed buying new clothes for herself in order to get new clothes for us children. She did these things joyfully, without complaining, and I began to realize that this must be a sensible way of life. She never coveted other people's houses, other people's servants, other people's cars — she was deeply joyful in that God had been so amazingly good to us.

Everything in the New Testament backs up and empowers the Tenth Commandment. The Christ on the cross was "wonderfully queer." Coming not to be ministered unto, but to minister, he washed the feet of his disciples. For the joy that was set before him, he endured the cross, and laughed at the shame. He came "that *they* might have life and have it fully." He taught us to love neighbor and to love enemy, and when we do this, envy has no place in the scheme of things.

Covetousness is greed: There is enough for the world's need; not enough for the world's greed. Edwin Poteat puts it: "Covetousness is desire drained of love." It is wanting more than my share. It is being content with injustice and unfairness. It is gathering to myself so relentlessly that I deprive others of necessities. It is a vicious game that men play and eventually leads to death.

Some persons who have great capacity for production should use this capacity to its fullest and, then, be wise enough to know how to use it for humanity's needs. It is even possible to covet one's own wealth and not share it. An old castle, The Mouse Tower, stands on an island in the middle of the Rhine River. This is its story: In a time of famine, its owner stored it full of grain, and refused to share it with his hungry neighbors. He held it for a higher price on his grain. But when he was ready to sell it, he discovered that the mice had invaded the tower and had destroyed his grain. He was left with nothing. It is sadly true that the greatest part of humankind prefer their own private good before all things. In coveting one's wealth, the great problem is: What is my share? How much can I lavish on myself? How much must I pour creatively back into life? "My share" cannot be determined by someone else, but is ultimately established by my own relationship to God. In many cases God has discovered that he could trust a person with a million dollars; in other cases he has found out he could not trust certain individuals with wealth. Business persons can either lose or find their souls in the use of their wealth.

Covetousness is an ancient poison that can be eradicated by an ultimate devotion to Christ. Cain coveted Abel's acceptance by God and he slew his brother. Joseph's brothers coveted his preferred relationship with their father and they sold him into slavery in Egypt. Once I stood on a barren hill in Northern Palestine and beheld the ruins of what was said to be the palace of Ahab and Jezebel. Quickly there flashed through my mind thoughts of Nabath's vineyard. The king had everything; yet, he was made sick because he coveted one little green spot that belonged to a poor man. Jezebel fulfilled Ahab's greed by having Nabath killed so that Ahab could possess the little garden. And the nation was doomed. Wrong desires, unworthy desires, and selfish desires can wreck your life in any country or any corner of the earth.

From time to time the Mafia gets into the news. How could a whole empire of murderous crime be established on man's greed, his weakness to desire something that does not rightly belong to him? We have seen how lobbies, unfairly used, can tie up a segment of our government so that justice breaks down and we fear for our future. There is enough wealth in the world to bring humankind physically to the abundant life; but wealth alone cannot do it. Wealth requires spiritual control, and the directive of the power of love. As the Christ Spirit conquers covetousness, human beings will live together in mutual caring and increasing creativity and joy.

Covetousness poisons human personality. We covet things; we envy people. It is just as dangerous to be green with envy, as to be purple with rage. Both produce stress, high blood pressure, headaches, strokes, ulcers, heart attacks, nervous breakdowns, and death.

Envy keeps us from laughing with those who laugh and weeping with those who weep. It defeats normal relationships and mutual caring. We become unhappy in the happiness of others; we become happy in the failure of others. Perhaps we need to be *less* content with what we are, and *more* content with what we have. Paul, possessed by the Spirit of Christ, could say: "I have learned in whatever state I am, therewith, to be content." Covetousness blocks us from "pressing toward the goal of the high calling of God in Christ." It prevents our "knowing the height and depth, the length and breadth of the love of Christ"; it detours us from "being rooted and grounded in love." It blocks our being "filled with all the fullness of God."

There is a Divine Covetousness: "as the hart panteth after the water brook, so panteth my soul after Thee, Oh God." There is a "hungering and thirsting after righteousness." There is an honest yearning for God, and "the unsearchable riches of Christ." Zacchaeus, the crooked tax collector, was a walking example of covetousness and greed. In a short walk with Jesus down the streets of Jericho he was set free — as he put it — "to give half of my goods to feed the poor"; to give back four times whatever he had taken unfairly. He was set free to live in the unlimited boundaries of love and caring, and his whole family was set free for great living.

Christ said that we are to love each other with the same kind of love with which he has loved the world. What's wrong with me? Why can't I do it? Why can't I at least begin to change, step-by-step? Why is change a threat to me when, in truth, it is my liberation, my entering into full *life*? Being "a new creation in Christ" might be exciting! Courage to change costs more than caution, but it promises more!

"Thou shalt not covet." It is possible, by the grace of God, to move from greed to generosity; from selfishness to the service of others. But there has to be a break! This is the threshold of Life Eternal.

---

1. Louis Charbonneau, *The Ice* (Thorndike Press, 1991), p. 320.

2. Anthony Burgess, *Earthly Powers* (New York: Simon and Schuster, 1980), p. 413.

Chapter 12

Christ-Love
Fulfills The Commandments

I imagine I was flying alone years ago. It was dark and stormy; my fuel was low. I was desperately seeking some place to land in safety, when I glimpsed yonder to the left a sweep of light, a flash of light, and the sweep again. I could breathe easily again; I was on my way to the runway. The light had beckoned me. I would survive. When I am morally and spiritually lost and am seeking a full life, there is the light of Christ and his love always calling me home to safety, joy, and fulfillment. The love of Christ is my guiding light.

The Ten Commandments say, "Thou shalt not hurt one another." Christ-Love says, "Thou shalt help one another." Jesus made it clear, "I came not to destroy the law, but to fulfill it." Then he gave us the Eleventh Commandment: "A new commandment I give unto you, that ye love one another; as I have loved you, that ye also love one another" (John 13:34). The new morality of Jesus breaks into the new dimensions of human relationships based on the ultimate demands of love.

Jean-Paul Sartre once wrote: "Hell is other people." Christ does not see it thus. A great anthropologist, Dr. Leakey, says, "One human being is no human being." None of us can be truly human in isolation. Christ eternally works on the basis of this reality.

Dr. Carl Jung, the great psychiatrist, writes: "Among all my patients in the second half of life, that is over thirty-five, there has not been one whose problem in the last resort was not that of finding a religious outlook on life … and none of them has really been healed who did not regain his religious outlook." Love is basic to health; it is basic to life itself.

But, at the moment, we stand with T.S. Eliot "in an age which advances progressively backwards." Pope Leo XIII states it this way: "Civil society was renovated in every part by the teachings of Christianity. In the strength of that renewal, the human race ... was brought back from death to life." The command of Christ that we love one another is the heart of that healing power. Jesus is alive and personal and here. When we deal with him, we deal with God. He is one of us, yet more than one of us. He fully represents God for our planet. Why can't we human beings realize this basic fact of life?

Each one must not forget that each is personally involved and personally responsible. Chaim Potok writes: "Even the master of the universe needs humankind in order truly to complete the creation." Think of that!

A great Christian friend said to me just before he died, "The spiritual is now more real to me than the physical. It is the only reality." To come a little closer to our own limited vision: there is a force at work in all of us, from the cradle to the grave and beyond. That force is love. It is God — it is eternal — it is mystery. When we yield to this force of divine love, and hold nothing back, we break into new dimensions of life, now and forever.

Without the love of Christ alive in our souls, we are possessed by envy, ambition, rivalry, hate, and greed; and without the benevolent control of the Christ Spirit we toil on to our doom. A character in a novel by Edward Rutherford cries out in desperation: " 'In the end, I was ready to take my own life. Only when I returned and found the love of my family did I once again desire to live. It is true therefore, what the preachers say: the world is good for nothing without love.' And gradually in his mind a new formula had taken shape: Life itself is love; death is lack of love. That is all there is to it."

Makkiya, the youth in *When Rain Clouds Gather*, was always running like so many youth are running today: "All his life he had wanted some kind of Utopia, and he had rejected in his mind and heart a world full of ailments and faults. He had run and run away from it all, and now the time had come when he could run and hide no longer and would have to turn around and face all that he had

78

run away from. Loving one woman had brought him to this realization." When love possesses we stop running and seek to work out the creative relationships demanded by love. Love is compelling and positive; love has dreams in it and structure; love is creative; love stops running away and faces up to life.

Law does not destroy love — it instructs it and guides it. Love does not destroy law — it interprets, corrects, and fulfills it. I am speaking of principles, not legalistic trivia and minutiae. "Behold the love of God that taketh away the sins of the world"; behold the love of man that taketh away the hurt of the world. Love stands at the door and knocks. Christian love is willing God's will, and thus overcoming man's disharmony. It is good to know that love comes from "Headquarters" — "God so loved the world!"

"There is a *wideness* in God's mercy." We see the riot in Los Angeles, the destruction of hurricanes, the deaths in Yugoslavia and South Africa and wonder if, instead, there is a *wildness* in God's mercy. William Sullivan shows us: "Thought, purpose, reason, logic, industriousness, but without the radiance of love: Isn't it an accurate description of *Satan*? These things are good. Men give themselves to these forces; but without love they become self-destructive. Without love, energy is surrendered to evil. Add love and God's counter-revolution is begun."

In the book, *A Child Possessed*, the character Stephen describes his resurrection from hate to love in a frightened prison camp experience: "That was when I tried to see where it came from, this power I had found in other men of deserting themselves, surrendering their own advantage. I hunted in my own nature … and there I saw nothing but a mixture of appetites of self-regard. Then one day I found myself crying with pity … for one of the guards … who had done me out of a day's rations … I had to look outside myself for the reason. And then I saw it quite plainly … I saw the goodness of God can only work by means of His creation … it can find a passage through every human absurdity and every corruption … I did — in those days of endless darkness — I did see God's goodness as a thing entirely different from anything I had learned or imagined. It was a waterfall of light, but it was also close and personal — not a vague and misty thing, but tangible."

God's counterrevolution had begun. Stephen rediscovered gentleness and compassion in relation with his retarded child. Through suffering, he rediscovered love for Helene, his wife.

Law without love is not sufficient; struggle without love is not adequate: "A new commandment I give unto you." Christ-Love does not offer the world a threat, but a hope! People try to improve human relations and only add more bitterness: In fighting the monster we become monsters. Force creates a counterforce that seeks to destroy it; love creates a counterforce that seeks to love in return.

There is a world of difference! Without love we are blind; we have thwarted our capacity for compassion; we have locked ourselves in the prison of self; we have become "walled towers built to face the winter skies"; we work with people, live with people, ride to work with people, live next door to people, and never know them as persons. We become capable of such facetious attitudes as: "Eva Lois, there is *something* here to see you; or, I'd just like to see you love *my* neighbors." A German prayer opens our eyes: "This is our poverty; we don't belong to each other, nor serve one another; we go each our own way and do not care what happens to our neighbors. We pray thee, O Lord, redeem us from this estrangement, redeem us out of this loneliness."

The world is waiting! The whole creation is groaning to see the manifestation of the Sons of God! To see Christ-Love breaking through to change the climate of human relationships. The Holy Spirit creates us in life; the Holy Spirit re-creates us in love. Love is the cure for our spiritual blindness. We love one person; we love those closest to us; we listen, we share, and in Christ-Love we find the way to the rest of the world. Love is ever open-ended, ever pulling us out into the new and creative: "A top without a top; a bottom without a bottom; a distance without an ending" — love is unlimited liability, unlimited possibility.

A recent article reveals the brighter side of today's youth. Larry Rockefeller, heir to great wealth, graduate of Harvard, has just completed three years as a "block worker" in Harlem. He lived in the slums and identified himself with the people; three years is a long time. He established a library. He set up a preschool. He helped people work out their problems and learn to help each other. They said of him: "Larry didn't do everything for no one. He helped us. Now people you could not talk to before will pitch in and help." Larry himself said: "Now I have an understanding of how deep and complex the problems are and how slow change comes, with great effort, and with how many setbacks."

In one of the songs of the new generation, we hear the cry: "Help! I need somebody. Help! Not just anybody. Help! You know I need someone. Help!" Christ-Love hears the cry and becomes the Breath of Life. We hear, we respond, and with J. G. Phillips we realize that "our cozy little world of doing good to those who know and like us suddenly enormously and painfully extended to all those who need our compassion and help … (far beyond) ordinary human niceness and kindness."

If God is Love and Christ is Love, that explains his power; if God is Love, and I do not love, that explains my emptiness. Simon Peter was a human, likable sort of a fellow; then he met Christ. He saw how Christ loved; he felt how Christ loved: A page was turned and the world opened wide. Peter became a new type of person; outsiders turned and looked at him. Under the "touch of Christ" our pages can turn! Our world can open wide! Otherwise it might be written in our epitaph: "This fellow, for lack of gifts and resolution, did comparatively little harm."

We agree with Boris Pasternak in *Doctor Zhivago*: "But don't you see, this is just the point — what has for centuries raised man above the beasts is not the cage but an inward music." This Christ-Love; this creative concern for people; this new vision of hope and promise is what Bertrand Russell once grudgingly admitted: "The root of the matter … The thing I mean — please forgive me for mentioning it — is Love, Christian Love, Compassion. If you feel this you have a motive for existence, a guide in action, a reason for courage, an imperative necessity for intellectual honesty." It is in this that today's youth, who have been running away, may turn and face it, and find themselves.

When you love people for Christ's sake they respond; then you love them because they are lovable. Love is not an easy morality; love is a tough morality. Love forgives others, but maintains a strong inner discipline. Love does not draw blueprints. It catches a glimpse of a new hope! It sees man's humanity to man. It sees (youth) exulting to grow and to build, taking responsibility for their homes, their schools, their communities, and their country. It hears a new kind of laughter, and such singing as comes only from the free-hearted.

It is good to *hope*! It is good to have *faith*! We do not need to wallow in misery because others are in misery — making misery total. By the grace of God, we can experience joy and share joy, until the world knows *joy*! There is something good about happiness. "This is our faith tremendous — our wild hope, who shall scorn — that in the name of Jesus, the world shall be reborn!" A New Commandment: "That ye love one another, as I have loved you." Impossible! Yet, we yield to him, in whom all things are possible!

The morality of the Ten Commandments, and Love — something old, something new. Both from God!